The Bethlehem Story

The Bethlehem Story

Mission and Justice in the Margins of the World

ANDY McCULLOUGH

Foreword by Jack Sara

Afterword by David Devenish

RESOURCE *Publications* · Eugene, Oregon

THE BETHLEHEM STORY
Mission and Justice in the Margins of the World

Resource Publications
An Imprint of Wipf and Stock Publishers
199 W. 8th Ave., Suite 3
Eugene, OR 97401

www.wipfandstock.com

PAPERBACK ISBN: 978-1-7252-6927-9
HARDCOVER ISBN: 978-1-7252-6926-2
EBOOK ISBN: 978-1-7252-6928-6

03/23/21

To the people of Bethlehem
A beautiful, hospitable, creative and resilient people.

إهداء
إلى أهل بيت لحم
شعب جميل ومضياف ومبدع ورزين

Contents

Foreword

Rev. Dr. Jack Sara,

President, Bethlehem Bible College

In an age like ours where the abundance of information has become almost a burden on people, and knowledge is available with one click in the palm of our hands, it becomes harder and harder to distinguish which knowledge and which information are true. Whose wisdom should I heed? To which channel should I subscribe? To what extent should the virtual realities of this world impact my beliefs and actions? I say this because somehow, in this book, Andy McCullough is addressing a topic that usually doesn't get any airtime within all of this world of information; a topic which, though overlooked, is vitally important.

As global citizens who ought to be concerned about our universe, sometimes it's not easy to refocus our attention onto a small place like Bethlehem. With all the global needs of today, Andy brings into focus a town that brought a Saviour that changed world history.

Jesus was not born in a vacuum. Rather, the town of Bethlehem was part of God's salvation plan and story from the beginning, and ancestors like Rachel and Ruth, and forefathers like David, are all knitted together into a beautiful account in Andy's book.

As Bethlehem today continues to be under the siege of occupation, economic crisis and the emigration of its children who feel, as Andy describes it, that they are "living on the wrong side of the world," there are enormous repercussions on the generations to come. All of us here fear that one day our Church of the Nativity might become only a museum or a worship place for pilgrims with no local Christians worshiping in it.

Certainly we do understand, as Andy also relates in his book, that zooming in on Bethlehem does not excuse us from seeing all the global challenges and problems and the suffering of other nations, but what happens in Bethlehem is a microcosm of things happening globally; the injustice, the silence of the church and the obnoxious attitudes of world leaders towards these issues. Too often, silence does more harm to the issues at hand than speaking out against injustice and the abuse of power and even the misuse of biblical texts. Andy works hard to help us to see various misappropriated texts from a different perspective.

In the pages that follow, Andy does great job of bringing biblical narratives into perspective. This is something that has really challenged me and I am certain that it will challenge those readers who want to grapple with truths that they are not used to hearing from popular writers, or Bible expositors that sometimes, sadly, want to tell us what we want to hear.

Another perspective that Andy portrays over and over is the culture of the Middle East that comes across when one studies the Scriptures. I love the way he talks about Rahab for example, who came as a refugee to Bethlehem. God took care of her and used her in an amazing way to be an integral part of salvation history. Like Rahab, tens of thousands of our people, the Palestinians, Muslims and Christians alike, have found refuge in Bethlehem. Bethlehem became a refuge to many, not only during the occupation of Palestine, but also in the aftermath of the 1915 Turkish genocide against the Armenians and other Christian minorities under their rule, when many Assyrian Christians fled to Palestine and most of them came to Bethlehem to seek refuge.

Drawing parallels between biblical narratives and current issues that are faced by peoples now, like the Palestinians or other minority groups, is certainly a skill that Andy has, and it is seen clearly in his writing. I believe Bible scholars and expositors could learn a lot from Andy as he shows us a prime example of what missiologists call contextualisation.

In conclusion, I have to say well done, Andy, for focusing your writing over and over again on the central Person, which is Jesus our Lord and Saviour. He is certainly the culmination of all the promises, the yes and amen. You have done right in making your exegesis and exposition point over and over to the Messiah, the author and finisher of our faith. In him and him alone we have salvation and to him and him alone be the glory, Amen.

Jack Sara
Bethlehem
Christmas 2020

Abbreviations of Ancient Sources

1QM	Dead Sea Scrolls: *1QWar Scroll*
1QS	Dead Sea Scrolls: *1QRule of the Community*
ActsPil.	*Acts of Pilate*
Ant	Josephus: *Jewish Antiquities*
B.Bat.	*Bava Batra*
Ber.	*Berakhot*
CD-A, CD-B	Dead Sea Scrolls: *Damascus Document*
Ces. Arles.	Cesarius of Arles, *Sermons*
Cont. Cel.	Origen: *Contra Celsum (Against Celsus)*
Cyril	Cyril of Jerusalem, *Catechetical Lectures*
De Spec.	Tertullian: *De Spectaculis*
Dial.	Justin Martyr: *Dialogus cum Tryphone (Dialogue with Trypho)*
Gen. Rabbah	*Midrash Rabbah: Genesis*
Haer.	Irenaeus: *Adversus haereses (Against Heresies)*
Jer. Ep. #	Jerome: *Letter #*
J.W.	Josephus: *Jewish War*
Or. Num.	Origen: *Homily in the Book of Numbers*
Pss. Sol.	*Psalms of Solomon*
Sanh.	*Sanhedrin*
Sheqal.	*Shekalim*
S.T.	Aquinas: *Summa Theologica.*

Ta'an	*Ta'anit*
T. Jon	*Targum Jonathan to the Prophets*
Tg. Ps-J.	*Targum Pseudo-Jonathan*
T. Jud.	*Testament of Judah.*

Introduction

Has not the Scripture said that the Christ comes from the offspring of
David, and comes from Bethlehem, the village where David was?

—JOHN 7:42

UP THE HILL TO Bethlehem. Through the military checkpoint and the
imposing "security wall"; concrete and barbed wire and hatred, which for
the last two decades has turned Bethlehem into something of an open-air
prison. Past the signs to Rachel's Tomb. Round the edge of Aida Refugee
Camp which still houses families who fled the 1948 *Nakba*, "The Catastro-
phe." Pause in the shade across the road from Banksy's *Walled Off Hotel*,
home of resistance art. Take photos of the powerful and disturbing images
and accounts that have turned the Palestinian side of the wall into a gallery
of injustice. Continue up Manger Street to the Church of the Nativity, the
birthplace of Jesus Christ. The holy mystery of Word-become-flesh is not
disconnected from the dusty, visceral realities one walks through on the
way up the hill. Indeed, Christmas is God's answer to weapons and walls
and refugee camps. God's self-contextualisation in Christ has a context.[1]
And that context is Bethlehem.

Bethlehem is the hinge of history. Tiny, carrying weight disproportionate to its size, often invisible, Bethlehem, like any good hinge, serves
humanity as the birth of Jesus Christ opens the door of heaven.

Why tell the story of Bethlehem? The writers of the Bible kept coming
back to this place as part of the unfolding revelation of God. This village
has a strong link with the ever-narrowing election-story: as a people, Israel;

1. Padilla, *Mission Between the Times*, 83.

1

as a tribe, Judah; as a family, David; as a descendant of David, Jesus Christ. Or, looked at from the other end of history, a significant number of the members of Jesus' genealogy, the messianic ancestors, had a relationship with Bethlehem.

There is a line that runs right through the story of Bethlehem to Jesus Christ. The story of Bethlehem is the story of Messiah, the anointed one, God's plan to save the world. The themes that adorn this complex and stunning story overlap and recur again and again. Bethlehem is a place of tears, of marginality and vulnerability, of hospitality and the embrace of "the other,"[2] of heroic women, of shame-removal. It is the birthplace of shepherds and kings. It stands against Jerusalem as a kind of prophetic counterpart, a rebuke to Jerusalem's fascination with power. These are all themes of Messiah. These are all vital aspects of mission. And they are all evident within five minutes of arriving in Bethlehem today.

Bethlehem's story is our story. We are in Christ, and Christ is from Bethlehem, from the tribe of Judah, from the line of David, from the union of Boaz and Ruth, of Salmon and Rahab. We have a spiritual stake in Bethlehem that is at least 3,000 years old. Her history is our history. Her families are our family.

That's why thousands of tourists and pilgrims flock to Bethlehem every year, to visit the Church of the Nativity, one of the holiest sites in Christianity. And yet her marginality persists. She is still a place of tears, a home of resistance art, a small town, overshadowed by Jerusalem, overpowered by empire. She is still the home of resourceful Palestinian women, as she has been since Rachel was buried there. She still welcomes refugees, is a model, although not perfect, of an ethnically diverse population. She is still a kind of permeable boundary between the populated land to the west and the desert to the east; in fact, she is physically a crossing-place through "The Wall" into the West Bank. There is much about the geographical and cultural realities of Bethlehem today that remain virtually unchanged. Getting to know Bethlehem will help us to better understand the story of the Bible, because the Bible pivots on Bethlehem.

I have never lived in Bethlehem. I have wanted to tell this story because I love the Bible, because I love people, and because I care deeply about God's world. Painfully aware of the limitations of my own particular social location, I have needed to spend several years studying, travelling,

---

2. "The other," throughout this book, will reflect the common human instinct to discriminate against those who are somehow different, the outsider, the foreign.

and listening to make sure that this book is rich enough to merit your consideration. Yet I've done little more than scratch the surface, than offer an introduction to a way of reading, a way of seeing. There have been times when this writing project has felt lonely, a voice crying in the wilderness, arriving at too many conclusions that might be considered alien by my own community. But, like the Judean wilderness east of Bethlehem, it is a populated wilderness. At times in the history of the Holy Land, people have *en masse* "gone out" from the towns and cities to seek the comfort and protection of the desert: they gathered to David in Adullam and to John the Baptist between Jerusalem and Jericho. In the first few centuries AD, it was common for urban Christians to renounce all and join a monastery in the same desert. Prophetic resistance is not lonely. Those who "go out" will always find a community who are learning what they are learning, seeing what they are seeing, and feeling what they are feeling.

And so this book seeks to tell the story of Bethlehem from four perspectives, from the perspectives of four communities. Any one of these strands on its own is too niche, too thin, too susceptible to misunderstanding. But I hope that, with the four taken together, my readers will go on a journey that combines discovery, beauty and instruction. These four perspectives arise from what I believe about the Bible: 1) the Bible is one big story (literary and biblical-theological approach); 2) the Bible is a Middle Eastern book (perspectives from the Middle East, particularly the dynamics of honour and shame); 3) the Bible is a global book (views from the margins of the world, and especially from contemporary Palestinian Christians); and 4) the Bible is a mission story (application to the mission of the church in our day). In what follows in this introduction, these four perspectives are expanded, so that the reader knows what they are getting themselves into. If you are not interested in methodology and just want to get into the story, then feel free to skip this introduction and jump right in.

THE BIBLE IS ONE BIG STORY

The Bible is God's big story, a grand narrative, with a beginning and an end, a hero and a villain, and, despite its multiple authors, genres, and contexts, it maintains a remarkable, Spirit-orchestrated unity. By "story," what is meant is not myth or fable, but rather a sweeping, epic history of the cosmos, punctuated by hundreds of smaller individual stories. Yet these individual stories are held together by narrative glue and canonical context—understanding where and when in the Big Story a smaller story takes place is vital to its meaning. Approaching the Bible through literary analysis is important in present Old Testament study,[3] and requires, "a close reading of the text in which one pays attention to the use, repetition, and arrangement of words, shifts in voices, deliberate verbal strategies that cause breaks, surprises, contrasts, comparisons, ambiguities, and open-ended wonderment in the text."[4] What becomes important is not merely what is said, but what is evoked, what is implied, the connections that the author creates with other parts of the Bible.

Biblical Theology is the discipline that explores this unity, often taking a series of themes and tracking their unfolding until they arrive at their fulfilment in the person of Jesus Christ. Leithart, who at the time of writing is one of the most popular Biblical Theologians, writes of the importance of this approach:

> Like great novelists, the biblical writers repeat a theme, word or image throughout a book, and it accumulates significance as it goes. Looking at the use of a word or image in chapter twenty-five without first tracing how the author has packed meaning into the word in chapters 1–24 is like seeing the end of a movie first. We might get some of it, but mainly we will be left confused.[5]

Likewise, Dempster, in his Introduction to *Dominion and Dynasty*, writes:

> This literary/theological approach has much promise, since, if it is the case that the Hebrew canon is also a Text with a definite beginning, middle, ending and plot, then the task of discovering a fundamental theme becomes not an exercise in futility but an imperative of responsible hermeneutics.[6]

This book does the same, but instead of a theme I am taking a place. Bethlehem will remain unmoved as the storyline of history evolves around it. The significance of place is important in the Bible. Geography is a vehicle for theology. Matthews calls this repeating of important places "geographic reiteration":

---

3. See Alter, *Art of Biblical Narrative;* Sternberg. *Poetics of Biblical Narrative.*

4. Brueggemann, *Jeremiah,* 15.

5. Leithart, *House,* 32.

6. Dempster, *Dominon and Dynasty,* 43.

Both historical reality and the familiarity associated with significant sites play a role in the expected setting of a narrative in order to give it or its characters greater authority. Whether it is transformed by sacred events or its strategic qualities, it thereafter becomes in the minds of generals, politicians, and biblical writers the logical site for future events. The repetition of geographic citation is based on both physical realities and the desire of those producing the account to add greater importance or traditional authority to the events of the story.[7]

For the Rabbis, geography was always an important part of interpretation. For example, the common tradition, represented by the *Targum Jonathan to the Prophets*,[8] draws a line from "The Tower of the Flock" (Hebrew *Migdal Eder*) in Genesis 35:21, to Micah 4:8, and the promised messianic ruler in Micah 5:2. As we will see in due course, *Migdal Eder* is a name for the shepherds' fields outside Bethlehem, where stone watchtowers for shepherds can still be seen today. The Palestinian Talmud combines Jacob's sheep-grazing and Micah's messianic promise in declaring that Messiah would arise from "the royal city of Bethlehem in Judah."[9] The early church father Origen was aware of this tradition, claiming that the Jews sought to supress the evidence for Bethlehem as Jesus' birthplace, lest he be considered Messiah.[10] This approach is not new. Place is important in the Bible.

Bull, writing about the Ruth story, zooms out to its setting in Bethlehem:

In Scripture, Bethlehem *is* critical. Review the events that cluster round it. We find it a city of coming and going, of life and death, of hopes and fears; a place of birth and departure; of anguish and delirious joy. There Benjamin arrives and Rachel goes. Elimelech vacates, and Ruth moves in. Mahlon and Chilion go forth and perish. Obed is nursed, and the ageing Naomi lives again. David's men risk all to serve him; a cup of water in his name. There Jesus is born. His star is shining; yet countless little children die.

---

7. Matthews, *Cultural World*, 40.

8. Targums are old Aramaic translations, with commentary, of the Old Testament. *Targum Jonathan to the Prophets* was probably written down in the second century, but reflects a much older oral tradition.

9. *Berakhot* 5a.

10. Vermes, *The Nativity*, 88.

The angels praise, the shepherds worship, then mother's eyes flow down with tears.[11]

It is not just that Jesus' birth in Bethlehem fulfils prophecy. The entire literary work of Scripture builds through cumulative geographic reiteration towards a Messiah born in Bethlehem, with all the associated meaning accrued over centuries. Jesus is the fulfilment of the Bethlehem story. In this book, then I am seeking to present a biblical theology of Bethlehem.

THE BIBLE IS A MIDDLE EASTERN STORY

Because the Bible is a Middle Eastern book, reading the Bible is a cross-cultural exercise, and time invested in seeking to understand Middle Eastern cultures can massively enrich, and, at times, correct one's reading of the Scriptures. This is particularly the case when it comes to the dynamics of honour and shame. Middle Eastern readings of Scripture, as Bailey has proposed, can give us "a place to stand as we attempt to escape the tyranny of our own cultural perceptions."[12]

These perspectives are especially instructive in our Bethlehem story. The horrifying concubine story in Judges 19 makes a little more sense if one understands the sacredness of hospitality as an index to godliness. The cost to Boaz' honour in redeeming Ruth makes us appreciate his sacrificial courage in moving towards her and absorbing her shame. The tribalism and vengeance in the David story make his peace-building with the tribe of Benjamin starkly counter-cultural. The danger to Mary's life as an unmarried pregnant girl and her narrowly-avoided honour-killing is often missed in the Christmas story. These are dynamics noticed by Middle Eastern readers of Scripture.

I have leaned-in to four kinds of sources to draw out the often unnoticed cultural dynamics in play in these stories. Firstly, I have listened to Middle Eastern Christians. Conversations, interviews, and interaction with published material are opening my eyes to the Middle-Eastern-ness of the Bible. Neyrey describes such cultural insiders as "guides": "A native Greek, Arab, or Spaniard raised in an honor-shame culture already knows the system which is expressed by these values, even if intuitively and unreflectively

11. Bull, *Love Song in Harvest*, 44.
12. Bailey, *Finding the Lost*, 39–40.

. . . we simply have no other way into this cultural world without such formal guides."[13]

Primary among these are Palestinian voices—Christians from Bethlehem to help us read the story of Bethlehem. Naim Ateek, the first to articulate a Palestinian theology of liberation, his student Mitri Raheb, founder of the Dar al-Kalima institute, brothers and sisters from Bethlehem Bible College and the Christ at the Checkpoint conference that is held in Bethlehem. I am hoping, through extensive footnoting, to introduce the reader to many of these, particularly as Palestinian Christians have been rendered "theologically invisible" as people who have kept the Christian faith in the land since the time of Christ. No-one asks their perspective. No-one listens to their opinion.[14]

The second bank of input comes from contemporary Jewish scholars. Yael Ziegler, Robert Alter, Tikva Frymer-Kensky, Jonathan Sacks, amongst others, feature greatly. Their insights into the nuances of biblical Hebrew and their cultural insider-ness to the Jewish tradition are outstanding.

Thirdly, Western missionary-scholars who have lived in the Middle East can really help the rest of the world see Jesus "through Middle Eastern eyes." In particular, the two Kenneths from last century, Kenneth Bailey and Kenneth Cragg, bring to the table decades of study, a grasp of languages, and a humble "living among," a listening approach that is instructive for any who seek to follow in their footsteps.

Finally, in the last thirty years much more has been written on honour and shame, and the cultural anthropology of the biblical world. Many of these authors are essential for those new to the subject. David DaSilva, Carol Meyers, Jerome Neyrey, Victor Matthews . . . their work is really helpful in guiding cultural outsiders through the social dynamics of biblical stories.

THE BIBLE IS A GLOBAL STORY

The power of the Bethlehem story is that Jesus Christ was born in a tiny village in the margins of the world. Bethlehem speaks to the disinherited, oppressed, colonised, those whose story is struggle and injustice and powerlessness. Bethlehem's story starts with Rachel being buried beside the road, "on the way," never really arriving or belonging, and this story is filled with refugees, stubborn survival, creative resistance.

13. Neyrey, *Matthew*, 6.

14. Raheb, *Empire*, 19.

Bethlehem actually is lived in by a people born on the "wrong side" of the world. "Palestinians did not lose merely their land. Those traumas also took away their language, their memory, their narrative, and their ability to tell stories," writes Bethlehem-born Mitri Raheb.[15] Modern Bethlehemites live under what they call colonial conditions, the Israeli occupation, but this is nothing new. Palestine, throughout its long history, has suffered repeated occupations and humiliations. Understanding this perspective, the perspective from the underside of history, will help the reader understand the Bible. Jesus was born under colonial conditions. Jesus was, for a while, a stateless person, forced to seek asylum in Egypt. Jesus was killed by the state machinery of an inflexible, oppressive, racist empire.

This is not just the Palestinian experience, but the experience of many minority peoples. Listening to Bethlehem, then, becomes a cipher for listening to many postcolonial voices, extending a microphone to the margins, exploring themes of justice and liberation and suffering. Bethlehem-born theologian Munther Isaac, in his recent book *The Other Side of the Wall*, uses the great concrete "security wall" surrounding Bethlehem and the West Bank as a metaphor for marginalisation: "Theology from behind the wall is viewing God and the Bible from the perspective of the marginalized and dehumanized."[16]

As I write, protests around the world respond to the brutal death of African-American George Floyd at the hands of a white police officer. Under the slogan #blacklivesmatter, hundreds of thousands are taking to the streets to protest institutional racism and perpetuated racial injustice. In Bethlehem, a mural of George Floyd has been painted on the wall, the great grey symbol of separation and empire, alongside pictures of Palestinian martyrs. #palestinianlivesmatter protests are taking place in Tel Aviv. There is a resonance and a solidarity between the black story and the Palestinian story. Indeed, the Bethlehem story speaks to any who, because of their ethnicity, find themselves on the wrong side of a wall of separation.

Listening is an art that requires discipline and concentration. Often, both what is said and the way it is said can seem too foreign to displace deeply-held subjectivities. We are too used to listening to views that refine and develop our already-embraced narratives, rather than views that subvert, challenge and provoke.

15. Raheb, *Empire*, 27.
16. Isaac, *The Other Side*, 20.

Within multi-centric Christianity, a multi-polar hermeneutic community[17] will help the church overcome ethnocentric blind-spots and demonstrate "the manifold wisdom of God" (Eph 3:10). We need each other, as Sri Lankan theologian D. T. Niles argued long ago, "The gospel is not safe in any culture without a witness within that culture from beyond itself."[18]

I can't articulate this better than Alison Phipps:

> To have a platform from which to speak as a teacher and as an understander of things, often of difficult things, is no small thing. In my work I try to share this space with those who are equally alert to and able to hold an audience but, by dint of their own migrations, have found themselves in contexts where their voices have not been heard, their accents have been shunned, their creative, skilful retelling of experiences in stories dismissed, their skin seen as too dark to suit the oh-so-white platforms of established power, except perhaps as a token embellishment. In these spaces we work to interrupt my own confident, rehearsed and experienced voice with other destabilising tonalities.[19]

This "view from the underside" is essential for understanding Scriptures that were written and preserved by minority communities, Jewish and Christian. It is also vital for the instruction of the post-Christian West, like the voice of older brothers who have been there and done it, "Here is how you survive as a minority. Don't panic that you are losing cultural power. Look to Bethlehem and find hope."

THE BIBLE IS A MISSION STORY

The story of the Bible is the story of God's great plan to fix what is broken and to transform the world. To quote Wright's now classic *The Mission of God*:

> *The whole Bible itself is a "missional" phenomenon.* The writings that now comprise our Bible are themselves the product of and witness to the ultimate mission of God. The Bible renders to us the story of God's mission through God's people in their engagement with God's world for the sake of the whole of God's creation. The Bible is the drama of this God of purpose engaged in the mission

17. Kessler, "From Bipolar to Multipolar Understanding," 458.

18. Niles, *Upon the Earth*, 166.

19. Phipps, *Decolonising Multilingualism*, 69.

of achieving that purpose universally, embracing past, present and future.[20]

Bethlehem is the launch pad of God's mission to save the world through Jesus Christ, the centre of this great rescue plan, the hinge of history. So where the repeated themes of the Bethlehem story re-circulate and re-percolate, there we find instruction about the *Missio Dei,* and therefore our own part in God's mission story. Bethlehem is hospitable to "the other," so should we be. Bethlehem welcomes refugees, so should we. Bethlehem is creative in peace-making and prophetic resistance, so should we be. Bethlehem is a place of solidarity and tears and incarnation, and that is the mode of the church's mission.

If Word became flesh, not in the centres of political power but in a tiny, vulnerable family in the corner of the world, then mission is a vulnerable, risky business. If lambs are born in Bethlehem to be sacrificed in Jerusalem, and the Lamb of God was born in Bethlehem in order to die at the hands of the temple elite, then disciples of the Lamb must also have an innocence, a readiness to be sacrificed. "Behold, I send you out like lambs amongst wolves" has always been a very Bethlehem rallying cry as Christ sends his people into the lions' dens of the world.

Mission means action, application, change. Reading this book should compel action. If Bethlehem weeps, then so do we. If Bethlehem, against all hope, survives, then so do we. If Bethlehem overcomes xenophobic impulse, so must we. If Bethlehem laments injustice, and takes a stand against empire, so must we. What we see in her story, we apply to our own stories. That's how biblical narrative is supposed to work. God is revealed through the story. We enter into Bethlehem's story with as much cultural and geographical colour and flavour as we can muster in order to feel the weariness of travellers seeking rest, taste the dust raised by occupying armies, hear the sheep bleating on the hillside. And there we find the Christ-child, son of David, Lion of Judah, Bread of Life, Lamb of God, Shepherd, Snake-crusher, fulfilling all the recurring themes of this epic story, taking his inevitable place as rightful king.

20. Wright, *The Mission of God,* 22.

1

Rachel
Death of the Beloved

Then they journeyed from Bethel. When they were still some distance from Ephrath, Rachel went into labour, and she had hard labour.

And when her labour was at its hardest, the midwife said to her, "Do not fear, for you have another son."

And as her soul was departing (for she was dying), she called his name Ben-oni; but his father called him Benjamin.

So Rachel died, and she was buried on the way to Ephrath (that is, Bethlehem),

and Jacob set up a pillar over her tomb. It is the pillar of Rachel's tomb, which is there to this day.

—GENESIS 35:16–20

JACOB'S FAVOURITE WIFE AND only true love, Rachel, dies in childbirth and is buried in a green place in the hills, just north of what would become our village of Bethlehem. This is Bethlehem's first appearance in the Bible. Rachel's tomb is still there today, well, just north of Bethlehem actually, on the

Hebron Road leading to Jerusalem. Jews, Christians and Muslims revere it as a holy site. Bethlehem, ever the place of tears, was founded on the death of the Beloved. Bethlehem's first landmark was a grave. Its first mention in Scripture is in a minor key. Bitter tears lubricate the hinge of history.

A sacrifice, Rachel dies that her son might live. And yet, as he is drawing his first breath and she her last, she cries out *Ben-Oni*—"Son of Sorrow!" What a name! Was she cursing with the pain of delivery? Or was she prophesying? Did she see, with a mother's instinct, all the trouble and pain that this child and his tribe would bring upon the people of God? "As her soul was departing" it seems she had a premonition of doom. Perhaps she foresaw that he would be the bane of God's people and would threaten the very Messiah for whom they were hoping. From Benjamin would issue the greatest persecutors, Saul of Gibeah and Saul of Tarsus. Benjamin would ever be a thorn in the side of the Seed.

Rachel, who had cried in her barrenness, "Give me children, or I shall die!" now, in bearing her second child, dies.

Jacob should have heeded Rachel's dying wish. In Genesis, mothers know their children better than their fathers do.[1] Jacob, however, is not prepared to accept these negative vibes about his son. He immediately, with Rachel's body still warm, re-names the baby *Ben-jamin*, "Son of my right hand," name of highest honour, name of inheritance, a King-name.

Jacob, bitter at having been tricked into marrying Leah, never had any intention of allowing the inheritance to pass to her sons. He desperately needed Rachel, her younger, prettier sister, to give birth, so that he could champion the favourite sons of his favourite wife. After years of waiting, Joseph's birth had been the trigger for Jacob finally to leave Laban's household and branch out on his own (Gen 30:25). "At last, I have a son through Rachel that can inherit my name," thinks Jacob to himself. "Now, at last, I can extricate myself from Laban and set up my own household of which I am the head." It's as though none of his previous ten sons counted for anything!

Jacob loved Rachel because she was so like him. Both were ambitious younger siblings who sought to gazump their older sibling. Both stole something from their fathers through trickery (Jacob, the birthright; Rachel, the household gods). Jacob loved Rachel, and despised Leah.

Jacob, in the blindness of love and favouritism, spends his life trying to transfer his inheritance away from Leah and all her sons. He has no

---

1. Sacks, *Covenant and Conversation*, 169.

right to do this.[2] Leah is the senior wife, and she produces the first-born son. But Jacob, seeking to break with culture and tradition, punishing Leah for being the cause of his embarrassment on his wedding night, when he was humiliated before the entire community, keeps trying to replace her as primary wife with Rachel. First, he re-names Ben-Oni. Then he gives Rachel's other son, Joseph the symbolic robe, leapfrogging him over all his half-brothers in the pecking order, provoking, inevitably, their virulent anger and jealousy. When they attack him, they are not just jealous of him as one of the brothers, but furious that as half-brothers their side of the family is being illegally disregarded. "Biblical co-wives, even blood sisters like Rachel and Leah, are such rivals that the Hebrew word for 'co-wife,' ṣarah, is also the word for 'trouble.'"[3]

In context, Jacob has just received a promise from God that "kings shall come from your own body" (Gen 35:11), and he has decided that Benjamin, son of his favourite, is destined for kingship. Without qualification or preparation. But the unfolding of Genesis will show us how wrong Jacob is. The Seed-line will come through one of Leah's boys, and all that Benjamin will produce is famous enemies of the Seed.

By promoting Rachel's two boys, Joseph and Benjamin, Jacob makes a terrible mistake. The promised King will come through Leah—the despised, unloved, overlooked, wife. Messiah, we learn, always proceeds from the un-preferred. In a world that is besotted with pretty Rachels, God is working through Leahs. Jacob didn't even want to marry Leah, and yet she is the Seed-bearer! Jesus comes from the ugly sister! The story of Bethlehem teaches us that God is Honourer of the Despised and Despiser of the Honoured, Chooser of the Unchosen and Seer of the Overlooked. As Palestinian theologian Naim Ateek puts it:

> Throughout the Hebrew Scriptures and the New Testament, God shows special concern for the underprivileged, the disadvantaged, and the vulnerable. This attribute of God, as concerned for the welfare of the weak, is not peculiar to one section of the biblical literature but is characteristic of the Pentateuch, the Prophets, the Writings, and the New Testament.[4]

---

2. In fact, Deuteronomy 21:15–17 would specifically forbid this.

3. Frymer-Kensky, *Women of the Bible*, 226.

4. Ateek, *Justice*, 130.

BURIED ON THE WAY

Rachel, we are told, was buried on the side of the road, close to Bethlehem. To be buried on the side of the road was highly unusual; almost everyone else in the clan was laid to rest at the family tomb in Machpelah. Rachel never arrived at this rest, she died and was buried "on the way," a symbol of non-arrival, statelessness, in-betweenness. The themes of "on-the-way-ness," exile, being far from home and not resting with one's fathers all combine to make Rachel a kind of patron saint of the dispossessed—which is the power in Jeremiah's and subsequently Matthew's referencing of her. In Jeremiah 31, on the eve of exile, Rachel is heard weeping for her children as they are marched off to Babylon in chains. She knows what it is to leave one's homeland, never to find rest.

> Thus says the LORD: "A voice is heard in Ramah, lamentation and bitter weeping. Rachel is weeping for her children; she refuses to be comforted for her children, because they are no more."
> Jeremiah 31:5

Matthew, narrating Herod's child-massacre in Bethlehem at Jesus' birth, again feels Rachel's anguish (Matt 2:18), as Jesus is made a refugee. Mary, like Rachel, travelled southwards in the late stages of pregnancy, giving birth at Bethlehem. In fact Mary, like Rachel, would be buried far from home, in Ephesus, with a shrine still visited by thousands of women annually seeking her blessing for family difficulties. Strickert, writing about Rachel, says, "She becomes a model for victims in various situations: the exiles heading to Babylon; the boy babies slaughtered in Bethlehem; and individual women struggling with motherhood and pregnancy."[5] Rachel is the first, but by no means the last, exile to be enfolded in welcome by Bethlehem's hospitable environs.

Of course, in a sense both women, Rachel and Leah, become forerunners of Messiah. Leah, through whom eventually Christ will come, is the rejected one. Rachel, buried close to Bethlehem, is the suffering one. Jesus was intimate with both rejection and with suffering.

5. Strickert, *Rachel Weeping*, xii.

RACHEL'S TOMB

The present structure known as Rachel's Tomb is not the pillar mentioned in verse 20, clearly. Today's domed building is an agglomeration of work by the Crusaders in the thirteenth century, Muhammad Pasha in the sixteenth century, and British Jew Moses Montefiore in the nineteenth. As Rachel is revered as a matriarch by all three great monotheistic religions, it seems fitting that all three have had a hand in preserving her resting-place. Devout Jewish, Christian and Muslim women have prayed at Rachel's tomb, particularly about family problems, for generations. Rachel in her repose has listened to her own agonised prayer, "give me children lest I die," repeated back to her countless thousands of times by desperate women seeking her patronage.[6]

Rachel is the first of many great ladies associated with the story of Bethlehem. In the biblical story we will meet Rahab, Naomi, Ruth and Mary. In the early centuries of Christianity, Constantine's mother the Empress Helena and Jerome's sponsor Paula will leave their mark upon this town. Bethlehem, from its very first mention, is a place of female courage, of maternal shelter and warmth, of nativity and new beginnings. Many of the sacred writings that we encounter during the Bethlehem story will associate this place with labour and birth: Micah 5:2, Isaiah 7:14, Luke 2:6, to name but a few.

Today, Rachel's Tomb is cut off from the rest of Bethlehem. You can't get there. The massive, concrete, 400-mile-long wall separating Jerusalem from the West Bank throws a loop around the Tomb, as it snakes across the landscape like a monstrous python. The barrier is eight metres high, a great grey symbol of distrust and unease, erected by the State of Israel in 2000.

Viola Raheb, a Bethlehem-born Palestinian Christian woman, agrees that Rachel's Tomb has always been a place where local women have gone to pray. In the last decade, however, access for Palestinians has been restricted by the Israeli forces. The tomb is now separated from Bethlehem by the wall and the checkpoint. "Rachel's Tomb as a religious site has been misused by the Israeli occupation and the ruling Israeli government to strangle Bethlehem,"[7] she complains.

On October 17th, 2000, thirteen-year-old Palestinian Muayad Jawarish was shot dead at Rachel's tomb, by a sniper positioned on top of the

---

6. Bowmann, "Weeping on the Road to Bethlehem," 169.

7. Raheb, "Reading Micah 5 in Modern Bethlehem," 65.

shrine. Frequently in recent history, Rachel's tomb has been a flash-point of protest. How painfully ironic that an icon of landlessness should be the focus of land-politics. And that a talisman of vulnerability should have been turned into something of a fortress, with 13-foot walls and armed guards.

> Rachel is the age-old symbol of the grieving mother. Her children are dying, Palestinian and Israeli alike. And Rachel continues to weep for them. Rachel cries, and so do Israeli and Palestinian mothers. . . . Inside the tomb, women wailing with tears over pregnancy and childbirth. Outside, mothers sobbing uncontrollably over the deaths of their sons.[8]

ON NAMES

There can be confusion about the place name Bethlehem, which in Arabic is *Beit Lachem* (House of Meat/Lamb) and in Hebrew is *Beth Lehem* (House of Bread). We will learn that Bethlehem is named House of Meat because it is the place where nomadic Arab shepherds come to sell their lambs, where Jacob grazed his flocks, where David tended sheep, and where angels declared to shepherds the birth of Jesus, Lamb of God and Shepherd-King.

And Bethlehem is the House of Bread because bread is a Semitic metaphor for kingship—kings provide bread for their subjects, hence a place of divine hospitality. Jesus, Bread of Life, come to feed a starving world, was born in the House of Bread, and placed in a manger—a feeding trough. It is as though God were saying, "*Bon apetit,* world! Come and feed on Him."

For Christians, both of Bethlehem's names, Hebrew and Arabic, are loaded with prophetic and symbolic meaning. The Lamb of God is born in the House of Meat, and the Bread of Life is born in the House of Bread.

The name of the region, given in verse 16, is *Ephrath,* which means "fertile." The villages of this district lie on a great aquifer in the limestone, making their hills verdant and their fruit trees lush. The contrast with the desert which starts immediately east of Bethlehem is absolute. Green on brown, as you look eastwards.[9]

The fertility of this region is legendary. The Ruth story takes place between the wheat and barley harvests. The fields of Beit Sahour to the east of

---

8. Strickert, *Rachel Weeping*, viii.

9. Gottwald, after discussing Ruth 1:2, 4:11, 1 Samuel 17:12, Genesis 35:19, and Micah 5:2, comments; "All the citations associate Ephrathah with Bethlehem." Gottwald, *Tribes*, 269.

the village were known for these crops.[10] Amos, who was from the neighbouring village of Tekoa, was a shepherd and a dresser of sycamore trees.[11]

Indeed, some historians argue that the name Bethlehem derives from the ancient fertility goddess Lachama. She was worshipped here long ago, in Ephrath, the place of lush fecundity, back around the time of Rachel's death in 1900BC. Deep in the collective memory of its residents, the themes of fertility, a matriarchal figure, and childbirth combine to make Bethlehem a place of supernatural fecundity. Especially when approached from the east, coming up through the desert from the Jordan valley, as the Israelites must have first done, to arrive in these hills is to be bowled over by abundance.

El-Khader, southwest of Bethlehem in the Ephrathah region, is also celebrated by association with St. George. The tradition of this dragon-slayer (another dragon-slayer from Bethlehem) also carries overtones of fertility. Fr. Methodius, the priest in charge of the shrine, explains: "All the Arabs—Christian and Muslim alike—call him "Khidr"—the Green One. The Palestinians think St. George can help give women babies or bring good crops to their fields or healthy lambs to their sheep."[12] Indeed, locally St. George's feast days are the fifth and sixth of May, coinciding with the grain harvest. On those days, worshippers buy bread from the village church, stamped with the St. George insignia. Here again, the themes of fertility, harvest and bread combine at the church of the saint.[13]

Bizarre as it may seem, the secretive English artist Banksy, who has been graffitiing on the wall as an act of protest since 2006, has opened a hotel directly across the road from Rachel's Tomb. The Walled Off Hotel (a pun on the famous Waldorf), which opened for business in 2017, is in touching distance of the wall, and popular with protest tourists. From the top floor you can catch a glimpse, over the wall with its machine gun emplacements, of the Matriarch's resting place.

Rachel weeps for her children. She is still weeping today. Her sons are still fighting each other. The wall around her tomb is a physical sign that all is not well. The desire to be top dog, as old as the hills, still dogs her descendants. Bethlehem is still a place of tears.

10. Raheb & Stricket, *Bethlehem 2000*, 109.

11. Amos 7:14.

12. Dalrymple, *Holy Mountain*, 340–343.

13. Marteijn, "Saint, Liberator, Martyr," 84.

Many of these themes will recur throughout the Bethlehem story. Motherhood and mourning. Birth and death. Exile and Refuge. This first biblical reference to Bethlehem prepares us for what is to come.

2

The Seed
Venom Absorption

> And I will put enmity between thee and the woman, and between thy seed
> and her seed; it shall bruise thy head, and thou shalt bruise his heel.
>
> —GENESIS 3:15 (KJV)

THE STORY BEGINS IN the garden. Celebrated as the *protoevangelium*, the first preaching of the gospel, God makes a promise to the snake. He tells the serpent, in no uncertain terms, how everything will end. Genesis 3:15 is read as part of the traditional Festival of Nine Lessons and Carols at Christmas. The Christmas story starts right here!

There are several key themes in this verse which will recur throughout the long journey to its fulfilment in a Bethlehem feeding-trough. The promise is of a snake-stamper, a dragon-crusher, a great hero who will emerge to end the tyranny of the deceiver. It is a promise of ultimate deliverance, final victory, the triumph of truth, the righting of wrongs.

HEAD AND HEEL

Yet this victory will come at a cost. As the foot of the deliverer comes down upon the head of the viper, the venom-laden fangs of the creature bury themselves into the heel of the stamper. In slaying the snake, the slayer is himself slain. The feet of Jesus are mighty enough to crush the head of the adversary, yet vulnerable to his mortal strike.

This theme, victory through self-sacrifice, absorption of evil on behalf of another, recurs through the generations of the Bethlehem story. It is an outstanding trait in all the Christ-types we will meet.

When Judah's half-brother Benjamin is accused of stealing the silver cup of the Egyptian, Judah offers himself on Benjamin's behalf: Let the snake bite me, let the boy go free (Gen 44:33). Boaz sacrificially marries the shameful outsider Ruth—he absorbs the shame associated with her. He decreases by association with her, she increases by association with him. The carpenter, Joseph, drinks the poison of the community's censure of the unmarried pregnant girl, Mary. By moving towards her, he steps into the firing line. He shelters her behind his broad shoulders.

All three of these, as well as others that we will meet, are venom-absorbers. All three teach us that salvation is through sacrifice. All three are associated with Bethlehem. All three are ancestors of Messiah. And all three point to Jesus, the One promised here. The Man whose death would be the ultimate victory.

SEED: SMALL, UNREMARKABLE AND BURIED

The second significant word here is the word translated "seed." Our other English translations translate it as "offspring," or "descendants," but the Hebrew *zera* or Greek *spermatos* bears the literal meaning "seed" as well as the metaphorical meanings "lineage, offspring, descendants, children."

> The Hebrew noun *zera* has the general meaning of "seed," which can be applied either in the agricultural sense or to human beings, as the term for semen. By metaphorical extension, semen becomes the established designation for what it produces, progeny. Modern translators, evidently unwilling to trust the ability of adult readers to understand that "seed"—as regularly in the King James Version—may mean progeny, repeatedly render it as offspring, descendants, heirs, progeny, posterity. But I think there is convincing evidence in the texts themselves that the biblical writers never

entirely forgot that their term for offspring also meant semen and had a precise equivalent in the vegetable world.[1]

Part of the power of the seed-concept is that a seed is tiny, unremarkable, and must be buried in order to produce results. The Bethlehem story, therefore, is a celebration of smallness. Scripture remarks on how unremarkable Bethlehem is—like in Micah 5:2, where the prophet expresses surprise that somewhere so insignificant could be the birthplace of someone so important. Many of the Seed-bearers in the messianic line are overlook-able individuals, such as Rahab the Jericho prostitute, Tamar the Dangerous (marry her at your peril!) and David the Eighth-born.

In a cashless agricultural society, seed is precious. Every year the farmer must gamble—how much of the harvest do I re-sow, re-invest for next year, how much do I turn into bread to feed my family this year? This is a gamble because in the changeable climate of the ancient Middle East so much could go wrong between sowing and harvest; the rains may not come at all, a crop-disease or locust invasion may ruin the crop, or marauding enemies may sweep through the land and steal the harvest at the point of the sword. Seed is a valuable commodity, but riskily sown.

Seed bears enormous multiplicative potential, but first it must be buried. Abraham, the ironically named "father of many," had only one son—one seed. But, having sown Isaac in faith into a death-and-resurrection type experience on Mount Moriah, Abraham ended up with seed as many as the stars in the vast dome of desert sky (Gen 15:5). Ultimately, according to Galatians 3:29, anyone from anywhere who belongs to Christ is now Abraham's seed. "Father of many" had one son. He buried him. And now he has millions. Jesus himself, the Seed of life, spoke of his own death in a riddle.

> Truly, truly, I say to you, unless a grain of wheat falls into the earth and dies, it remains alone; but if it dies, it bears much fruit. Whoever loves his life loses it, and whoever hates his life in this world will keep it for eternal life. John 12:24–25

The Father of creation had one son. He buried him. And now he has millions. These seed-dynamics are vital for understanding the messianic narrative. Messiah, declares our story, is like a seed. He must be small. He must be unremarkable. And he must be buried. Messiahs that are too big, too eye-catching or too indestructible are no messiahs at all.

---

1. Alter, *The Hebrew Bible*, xvii.

Small, unremarkable, and buried. And also slow. Everything to do with seeds is slow. Between sowing and reaping, an age. Middle Eastern farmers are some of the most patient people I have ever met. Bethlehem people seem to have a resilience, a stickability. This town, despite all that has been inflicted upon her in her millennia-long history, is still here, and she still has hope.

This promise, in the first pages of the Bible, when the world was still young, is like a seed. Small, easily overlooked, and thousands of years buried until its fulfilment in Christ. Eventually, three thousand years later, the Bread of Life is born, in the House of Bread, from this Seed-prophecy. That really is slowly baked! The Bible is not quick to get to Jesus, but in the waiting there are beautiful evolutions in the narrative, as the place and time and nature of the Bread of Heaven are kneaded together and left to rise.

Prophetic words are often like seed—they bear enormous potential but are hidden in our hearts until their fruition. The gospel is like seed, Jesus taught his disciples. And sometimes, according to Matthew 13, the gospel-bearers, we Christians, are like seed, sown into the world, small, easily missed and under the surface, slowly and quietly bringing forth the harvest of the Kingdom.

THE STORY OF THE SEED

We can track the Seed-story all the way from Genesis to Revelation. Eve is told here that the promised Seed will be a child of hers—will be a human. When she produces Cain she celebrates by naming him "Produced"—"See, I've produced the Seed!" although the Seed-line was to come through Seth—the Bible is explicit about this in 4:25. In Genesis the Seed-promise is repeated to Noah (9:9), Abraham (12:7, 13:15–16, 15:5, 17:7–10, 22:17–18), Isaac (26:3–4), and Jacob (28:13–14). The question throughout the second half of Genesis is "which of Jacob's motley bunch of sons will be the Seed-bearer?" The promise passes to his fourth-born, Judah, the first three having disqualified themselves, just as later it will pass from David to his fourth-born Solomon. Eventually, as Paul argues at length in Galatians 3, the Seed-promise is fulfilled in Christ. Again, the KJV preserves the meaning:

> Now to Abraham and his seed were the promises made. He saith not, And to seeds, as of many; but as of one, And to thy seed, which is Christ. Galatians 3:16 (KJV)

Consequently, those who are in Christ are also the seed of Abraham.

> And if ye *be* Christ's, then are ye Abraham's seed, and heirs accord-
> ing to the promise. Galatians 3:29 (KJV)

The Bethlehem story traces this Seed-promise through sacred history until its fulfilment in Jesus Christ, who was born of a woman in order to crush the snake.

THE SNAKE

Another leading word arising from Genesis 3:15 that will recur in various iterations throughout the Bethlehem story is snake. The Seed of the woman will constantly be harassed, persecuted, obstructed by the seed of the snake. This enmity will continue from generation to generation, until the ultimate and final head-crushing occurs. Thus, throughout the Bethlehem story, the snake will also make appearances in various guises. Hope is often articulated as viper-stamping, as in Psalm 91:13, Luke 10:19, or Romans 16:20, which reads:

> The God of peace will soon crush Satan under your feet. The grace
> of our Lord Jesus Christ be with you. Romans 16:20

An old Aramaic version of Genesis 3:15 (*Targum Pseudo-Jonathan*), interprets seed corporately, as the people of God. "When the children of the woman keep the commandments of the law . . . they will strike you on the head. But when they forsake the commandments of the law you will . . . wound them in the heels. . . . For them, however, there will be a remedy; and they are to make peace in the end, in the days of King Messiah."[2] This corporate understanding makes sense—it's not just that the one snake fights against the one Seed, but that snake-people oppose Seed-people all the way through Scripture. To be part of the Seed-story is to have an enemy. Bethlehem people are often harassed and surrounded. Indeed, that is their normal.

THE WOMAN

The promised One will be the descendant of Eve (the mother of the living); he will be the true human, true living one (Rev 1:18), born of a woman. In

---

2. *Targum Pseudo-Jonathan* on Genesis 3:15.

the very next verse, God turns from the snake to the woman and tells her, "I will surely multiply your pain in childbearing." The promised victory will only come through suffering.[3] Mothers, pregnancy, labour and birth will play a disproportionate role in the Bethlehem story. As we have already seen, Ephrathah means "fertile" and Bethlehem's geography renders it fecund relative to its surroundings. In similar vein, many of the women associated with the Bethlehem story are extraordinary mothers with extraordinary stories. These messianic mothers, such as those named in Matthew's and Luke's genealogies, are essential to the story of the world. The Bible, written in a patriarchal world where lineage was defined by male characters, repeatedly breaks with convention by tracing the female contributors to the mighty ancestry of Christ.

And Christ himself is born of a human mother, not a human father, in direct fulfilment of Genesis 3:15. Many of the early Fathers loved this idea. For example, Irenaeus in the second century: "The knot of Eve's disobedience was loosed by the obedience of Mary. For what the virgin Eve had bound fast through unbelief, this did the virgin Mary set free through faith."[4] And Cyril of Jerusalem in the fourth century: "Death came through a virgin, Eve. It was necessary that life also should come through a virgin."[5]

These themes reverberate all the way through the story of Bethlehem. We will meet women who have babies who do battle with snakes. We will face enmity. There will be persecution, as feet are bruised by snakes. We will see self-sacrificial suffering, absorption of various venoms, and we will see victory; partial victories over the snake as generation upon generation of Seed-bearers contribute their stories to the big story, like relay runners carefully stewarding their portion of Seed to pass on to their children. And, in Jesus Christ, ultimate victory as the Snake is once-and-for-all crushed, as the Living One is slain, as the Seed is buried, and, with the resurrection, as a new and snake-less garden emerges, as a new and suffering-less creation comes forth.

---

3. In particular, Isaiah will speak of labour pain in an eschatological sense (26:16–18, 54:1, 66:7–9), as Zion travails to brings forth Messiah, and with him New Creation.

4. Irenaeus, *Against Heresies* 3.22.4.

5. Cyril of Jerusalem, *Catechetical Lectures* 12.15.

3

Judah
Lion-Lamb

The sceptre shall not depart from Judah, nor the ruler's staff from between his feet, until tribute comes to him; and to him shall be the obedience of the peoples.

—GENESIS 49:10

FOURTH-BORN IS NOTHING, REALLY. Growing up, Judah would not have expected any special treatment. The Seed-Promise has passed from Abraham to the miracle child Isaac, from Isaac to the younger twin Jacob. At every step the transition has been unpredictable, sovereignly-ordained, unlikely. And now Jacob has twelve sons by two wives and two concubines. And the great question of Genesis needs to be answered—through whom will the Seed come? Judah, fourth-born, seems a most unlikely choice.

Reuben is first in the queue. Firstborn of Leah, the senior wife—prime candidate. But Reuben is impatient and ambitious. He tries to snatch pole position by sleeping with his father's concubine—an act of treachery, making a play for the throne, laying claim to his father's possessions while he is still alive. In the narrative flow, Rachel has just died and Jacob has unfairly elevated Benjamin with a king-name. Reuben, for fear of his rightful claim being gazumped, makes his move (Gen 35:22). He dishonours his father, and as a result will be written out of the will.

Sons number two and number three are Simeon and Levi. They also dishonour their father, this time by directly disobeying him, and ruining the family's good name in the process. When their sister, Leah's daughter Dinah, is raped they avenge her violently, expunging the dishonour through the shedding of blood, following the law of Lamech, who stipulated revenge at a ratio of 1 to 77. They try to show leadership and responsibility, but in the end are no different from the surrounding nations. It is possible that they feel Jacob will not do the right thing because Dinah is Leah's daughter, and Jacob has made it clear that his preferences lie with Rachel. In truth, Jacob is anxious because the embryonic people of Israel are a vulnerable minority who do not have the luxury of provoking the many enemies who encircle them. The way of meekness would have been wiser. Simeon and Levi, for this action, also are disqualified.

Fourth in the pecking order is Judah. Judah doesn't seem much better than his three failed brothers. He is complicit in the attack on Joseph—it is his idea to sell Joseph to the Ishmaelites—and afterwards, from shame and guilt, he separates himself from his brothers and ends up living in Chezib (which means deception), married to a Canaanite. Judah seems as much a failure as Reuben, Simeon and Levi.

Then Tamar steps into the story. Like Rahab and Ruth after her, she is a foreign woman in the messianic line who is explicitly named and honoured in Matthew's genealogy of Jesus.

I have told Tamar's story more fully elsewhere.[1] After Er and Onan die, it is Tamar's cultural right to be given to their brother Shelah, but Judah denies her this right. She is unjustly treated, the object of all the verbs and the subject of none, until verse 11 when, sent away, she becomes the actor. Tamar does what she can with the limited resources available to her and pursues conception by another male of this family, this time Judah himself. In disguise, she seduces Judah. When Judah needs to leave Tamar a pledge, he hands over his staff. This was not only a sign of identity, but of his authority—it was a shepherd's staff. This surrender of his God-given shepherding authority is the lowest point in Judah's life.[2] He has sold his younger brother into slavery and failed to take responsibility for his

1. McCullough, Global Humility, 17–23.

2. Testament of Judah, 12.

daughter-in-law. He has failed in his shepherding of the vulnerable sheep under his care. Like Esau giving up his spiritual inheritance for a fleshly desire, so Judah here has forgotten what is truly important.

When Judah is ready to condemn Tamar for her illegitimate pregnancy, Tamar confronts Judah, shows him his staff, calls him to account, turns him around. The margins correct the centre. The weak shames the strong. This woman makes a man of Judah. He publicly confesses his sin.

> "She is more righteous than I, since I did not give her to my son Shelah." Genesis 28:26

"This is the first time in the Torah someone acknowledges their own guilt. It was also the turning point of Judah's life . . . Judah is the first penitent . . . in the Torah," writes Rabbi Sacks.[3] According to Dempster,

> This text highlights two factors: first, the progeny of Judah through a Gentile woman, who wanted blessing for her dead husband. She was more righteous than the chosen people to whom she was related in marriage. She believed more in the seed than they did, and if it had not been for her ingenuity the promise would have been lost. But there is a second irony. The staff left with Tamar as a pledge of payment for sex becomes not only a means of evoking Judah's confession but the means by which *Judah will rule the nations in the future.*[4]

And the child that they have together forces his way out first, even though he was going to be born second to his twin brother. And he is named Perez, "Breach-maker," like his mother, who made a breach in her death-like widowhood and forced her way out, taking off her widow's garments and taking command of her own destiny. Like Perez' great descendant Jesus Christ, who would refuse to surrender to the tomb but forced his way out that glorious Sunday morning. Tamar made a breach in her fate. Perez made a breach in the womb. And Jesus made a breach in death!

Tamar is the latest in the Seed-bearing mothers to show the characteristics of wit, determination, unconventionality and courage. These marginal mothers become central to the story of Messiah through their own resourcefulness. The previous three generations, Sarah, Rebekah and Leah, each have something in common with Tamar. Sarah was wrongly given away when the patriarch felt threatened (by Abraham to Abimelech), just

---

3. Sacks, *Covenant & Conversation*, 313.
4. Dempster, *Dominion and Dynasty*, 90.

like Tamar. Rebekah veiled herself (Gen 24:65), and then used deception and disguise (Gen 27:6–16), and was a mother of twins, just like Tamar. Leah disguised herself in order to marry into the Seed-line, just like Tamar. These repeated themes are not incidental to the story of Bethlehem, as Frymer-Kensky points out in her study of these remarkable biblical women:

> The great-grandmother, the grandmother, and the mother of Judah overcame vulnerability and powerlessness to give birth to and determine the success of the grandfather and father of Judah and of Judah himself. Tamar continues this pattern to the next generation. They all were prepared to risk scandal, humiliation, ostracism, or death to have children with their families. They all were assertive and proactive, and each of them engaged in unconventional sexual activity to accomplish their purpose.[5]

Similar themes will emerge with Ruth and Bathsheba, who, like Tamar, are in addition outsider women brought in. Rabbi Sacks confessed that he found it "exceptionally moving that the Bible should cast in these heroic roles two figures at the extreme margins of Israelite society: women, childless widows, outsiders. Tamar and Ruth, powerless except for their moral courage, wrote their names into Jewish history as role models who gave birth to royalty – to remind us, in case we ever forget, that true royalty lies in love and faithfulness, and that greatness often exists where we expect it least."[6]

David, later, will show many correspondences with Tamar. Both disguised themselves when needed. Both showed someone in power over them something that belonged to them as a matter of life or death: Tamar to Judah the staff and seal, followed by Judah's pronouncement "she is more righteous than I." David to Saul a piece of his robe, followed by Saul's announcement "you are more righteous than I" (1 Sam 24:17). *Perez* or "breakthrough" is a word well associated with David. David named *Baal Perazim* "Lord of the breakthrough" in 2 Sam 5:20–22, and *Perez Uzzah* in 2 Sam 6:8.

Why does Matthew include these four Gentile women, Tamar, Rahab, Ruth and Bathsheba in the genealogy of Jesus? For St. Jerome, they were all obviously sinners, and hence the grace of God to sinners is on display, an idea which Aquinas affirmed, stating that the genealogy includes "only those whom Scripture censures, so that he who came for the sake of sinners,

---

5. Frymer-Kensky, *Women of the Bible*, 276.

6. Sacks, *Covenant & Conversation*, 269.

by being born of sinners, might blot out all sin."[7] However, the Old Testament narrative nowhere censures these women. In fact, they are honoured and celebrated in the Scripture.

Luther felt that they were included because they were all Gentiles. Matthew, in his first chapter, is setting out his stall to argue that in Christ, outsiders are brought in, just as these women are introduced to the family of the Messiah. Brown goes further, to suggest that these ladies are there to set the reader up to accept Mary's story. These women all share two elements in common with Mary. Firstly, "there is something extraordinary or irregular in their union with their partners—a union which, though it may have been scandalous to outsiders, continued the blessed lineage of the Messiah."[8] Secondly, "the women showed initiative or played an important role in God's plan and so came to be considered the instrument of God's providence or of His Holy Spirit."[9] To these two elements we could add a third, that they all have an association, through marriage, with Bethlehem.

JUDAH AS OLDER BROTHER

Judah, confronted and transformed by Tamar, now begins to play the role of older brother, of responsibility-taker. When Jacob is reluctant to send Benjamin down to Egypt, for fear of losing Rachel's only surviving boy and his nominated heir, Judah offers his own life as surety for his half-brother.

> I will be a pledge of his safety. From my hand you shall require him. If I do not bring him back to you and set him before you, then let me bear the blame forever. Genesis 43:9

This is an incredible development. Judah pushes past the rivalry and animosity between the two sides of the family and offers his own life on behalf of Benjamin. This is a peace-making initiative, overcoming decades of fierce animosity on both sides. Jacob must have been staggered by this unexpected offer! Then, even more dramatically, Judah steps into the firing line again on Benjamin's behalf, this time in Egypt before the regent.

> For your servant became a pledge of safety for the boy to my father, saying, "If I do not bring him back to you, then I shall bear the blame before my father all my life." Now therefore, please let

7. *Summa Theologica*, v. 5. p. 3 Q. 31.

8. Brown, *Birth of the Messiah*, 73.

9. Brown, *Birth of the Messiah*, 73.

your servant remain instead of the boy as a servant to my lord, and
let the boy go back with his brothers. Genesis 44:32–33

"You punish me, let the boy go free. Take me in his stead, in his place."
Joseph's carefully-constructed scene—whereby the sons of Leah again have
the opportunity to abandon a son of Rachel to slavery (this time Benjamin
instead of Joseph), having heaped food on Benjamin's plate (Gen 43:34)
to provoke them to jealousy (just like Joseph's special treatment by his father)—is designed to test whether or not they are repentant, whether they
have changed. Judah's response in this situation shows how much he has
changed. Presented with an overwhelming temptation to repeat the crime,
and to be rid of Rachel's progeny once and for all, Judah acts heroically.

> It is a precise reversal of character. Callousness has been replaced
> with concern. Indifference to his brother's fate has been trans-
> formed into courage on his behalf. Judah is willing to suffer what
> he once inflicted on Joseph so that the same fate should not befall
> Benjamin.[10]

This self-sacrifice, this voluntary self-substitution, offering himself
for the salvation of his brother, will be what ultimately qualifies Judah for
leadership. The narrator forges a link between the two pivotal moments
in Judah's story through the use of "pledge." Tamar compels Judah to give
a pledge, and Judah volunteers his own person as the pledge for Benjamin (Gen 43:9, 44:32–34). Judah, like his great descendant Jesus Christ, is
prepared to "bear the blame before his father." Where Benjamin had been
honoured by his father seemingly arbitrarily when he was given his name,
Judah humbles himself as the substitute for Israel gone wrong, as symbolised by Benjamin. Benjamin will continually bring trouble to Israel, and
Judah will continually rescue! Leithart identifies this trajectory:

> The distinction between a king from Benjamin and one from Judah
> is deeper than mere tribal associations; Benjamin was identified as
> a future king in Genesis 35 without any preparation or training,
> while Judah was proclaimed the royal tribe only after he had of-
> fered himself as a substitute for Benjamin. Similarly, Saul became
> king without ever accepting the cross, while David, the king from
> Judah, rose to the throne only after a death and resurrection.[11]

10. Sacks, *Covenant & Conversation,* 313.

11. Leithart, *Son to Me,* 76.

This comparison by Leithart will be re-visited in due course. David will demonstrate the same "death and resurrection" pattern as his ancestor Judah and as his great descendant Jesus Christ. In what is considered one of the oldest extended passages in the Bible,[12] Genesis comes to a climax with Jacob's sons gathered around his deathbed, the patriarch solemnly distributing spiritual blessings to them in age order. Is there an eschatological note to these prophetic promises, as Israel speaks of "the last days?"[13]

Reuben, as first-born, is first to receive his prophecy.

> Unstable as water, you shall not have pre-eminence, because you went up to your father's bed; then you defiled it—he went up to my couch! Genesis 49:4

He is passed over. He is not the Seed. He has disqualified himself. Next up are Simeon and Levi. They too are disqualified. And then it is Judah's turn. Old Israel turns to his fourth-born. Rashi, the mighty eleventh-century Jewish scholar, captures the drama of the moment, "In as much as he had heaped condemnations on the previous ones, Judah began to back away and his father called to him with words of encouragement, 'Judah, you are not like them.'"[14]

> "Judah, your brothers shall praise you; your hand shall be on the neck of your enemies; your father's sons shall bow down before you. Genesis 49:8

This promise is rich with word-play. "*Yehuda*, your brothers shall *yadah* you, your *yad* shall be . . ." the same sound repeated three times in different ways. Judah is given pre-eminence over his brothers. He is appointed leader.

In verse 9, Judah is depicted as a lion. This is the first of many references to the famed phrase Lion of Judah. Most famously, this phrase will be used in Revelation 5:5–6 of Judah's great descendant Jesus Christ. "Behold," John is told, "the Lion of the tribe of Judah, the root of David, has conquered." When John turns to look, however, he sees a Lamb standing "as though it had been slain." John looks for a Lion and sees a Lamb. The victory of the Lion is achieved through the sacrifice of the Lamb. What John describes in Revelation is what Judah learnt in Genesis, that laying

---

12. Alter, *The Five Books of Moses*, 192.

13. Genesis 49:1. This phrase recurs in other key messianic-eschatological passages.

14. Alter, *The Five Books of Moses*, 194.

down one's life for one's brothers is the crux of leadership, the locus of love, the hinge of history.

In verse 10, an international kingship is promised.

> The sceptre shall not depart from Judah, nor the ruler's staff from between his feet, until tribute comes to him; and to him shall be the obedience of the peoples. Genesis 49:10

Key messianic words circulate in this verse. The "sceptre" is Judah's shepherd's staff (*shevet*) become a token of kingship. This, by the time of Psalm 2, becomes strongly linked with Messiah, who is a shepherd-king. The "obedience of the peoples" will belong to him. Placing "feet" as a symbol of rule recalls Genesis 3:15. Judah receives the Seed-promise, the promised deliverer will come from his tribe.

It seems, from the chronicler, that Jacob still passed his technical birthright to Joseph and his sons (Rachel's line), but that divinely-ordained leadership stayed with the tribe of Judah.

> The sons of Reuben the firstborn of Israel (for he was the firstborn, but because he defiled his father's couch, his birthright was given to the sons of Joseph the son of Israel, so that he could not be enrolled as the oldest son; though Judah became strong among his brothers and a chief came from him, yet the birthright belonged to Joseph). 1 Chronicles 5:1–2

Japhet explains that there were three degrees of pre-eminence: "the biological firstborn, the legally nominated elder, and the one who wielded actual authority."[15]

Each tribe receives from their father their *sigil*, or logo, the brand that will identify them throughout the story of Scripture. Reuben's is water. Judah's is the lion. And Benjamin? Benjamin's *sigil* is a wolf.

> "Benjamin is a ravenous wolf, in the morning devouring the prey and at evening dividing the spoil." Genesis 49:27

The final word on Benjamin in Genesis shows that Jacob has at last understood what Rachel was trying to tell him with her dying breath. From Benjamin will come the greatest persecutors of the Seed. Saul of Benjamin will pursue David of Judah. The nation will be plunged into civil war along the fault line between these two tribes. And, far into the future, another Saul from the tribe of Benjamin would be the most famous wolf of all,

15. Japhet, *I & II Chronicles*, 133.

persecuting the Lion of Judah, Jesus himself. Judah's response will always be to offer himself as a sacrificial lamb, to seek not revenge or retaliation but reconciliation. Judah will ever be the venom-absorber. Saul, later Paul, will eventually understand this, writing of "the son of God who loved me and gave himself for me" (Gal 2:20).

4

Balaam
The Star and the Sceptre

I see him, but not now;
>I behold him, but not near:
>a star shall come out of Jacob, and a sceptre shall rise out of Israel;
>it shall crush the forehead of Moab and break down all the sons of
Sheth.

—NUMBERS 24:17

UP THE HILL TO Bethlehem came the wise men, the words of Balaam ringing in their ears and in their hearts.

Balaam was a professional pagan diviner with an international reputation. One of his non-biblical prophecies, dated 800BC, is preserved in an
Aramaic text from Deir Alla in the sweltering Jordan valley. Fabiola, one
of Jerome's female correspondents, asked him, "how came it to be that the
soothsayer Balaam, in prophesying the future mysteries of Christ, spoke
more plainly of him than almost any other prophet?"[1] A great question!

1. Jerome, Letter 77:7.

34

Is it possible to re-construct the connection between Balaam's remarkable messianic prophecy of the star and the sceptre, and Matthew's equally mysterious magi from the East?

Balaam, of Aramean ethnic extraction (Num 23:7)[2] was commissioned by the king of Moab to curse Israel as they passed through Moabite territory on their journey towards Canaan.[3] In Numbers 22:7–21, in what reads like a stereotypical bartering scene, Balaam, after initially refusing, allows himself to be persuaded to take up the contract. But his reluctance appears to be more than just negotiation acting. He seems genuinely uneasy about taking on this assignment, about cursing this people. God's promise to Abraham, rich with the language of blessings and curses, underlies much of the Balaam sequence in Numbers 22 to 24.[4] Curses are turned to blessings. And after three abortive attempts, with attempted curses becoming blessings mid-flow, the king of Moab's "anger was kindled against Balaam, and he struck his hands together" (24:10). Balaam is summarily fired for failing to fulfil his contract. Balaam answers, "I told you right at the beginning that this wasn't going to work." Prophecy is un-contractable. The Spirit of God is un-employable. God's blessed Seed, un-cursable.

And Balaam, dignity unruffled, gazing out across the vast plains at the ragged pilgrim people, gathers himself for one last burst. This final prophecy will be different—not just the blessing of Israel, but the impact that it will have on Moab. This oracle will be significant for the Bethlehem story, but also significant in Moab's story.

> And now, behold, I am going to my people. Come, I will let you know what this people will do to your people in the latter days.
> Numbers 24:14

This phrase, "the latter days" often refers forward to the messianic future.[5] We most recently encountered it in Genesis 49:1.[6] The king, the elders, all their retainers are present. There are court recorders on hand to write down what is pronounced, as there are everywhere the king goes. Royal scribes will capture this oracle. Most probably Balaam has his own

---

2. Layton, "Whence Comes Balaam?" 48.

3. See also Numbers 31:8; Joshua 13:21–22.

4. Schreiner, *The King in His Beauty*, 76.

5. e.g. Jeremiah 48:47; Daniel 10:14.

6. Also, as in Genesis 49, there is an almost verbatim "he crouches down like a lion, like a lioness . . ." (Numbers 24:5–9).

secretaries as well, to inscribe his words for posterity. High on the hill he lifts his noble, turbanned head, his strong aquiline features silhouetted against the spotless blue sky, gathers his flapping cloak and skirts around him, and begins to declaim in the guttural tongue of the ancient Near East:

> I see him, but not now;
> I behold him, but not near:
> a star shall come out of Jacob, and a sceptre shall rise out of Israel;
> it shall crush the forehead of Moab and break down all the sons of
> Sheth. Numbers 24:17

Remember, he has been paid to prophesy by the king of Moab. Yet here he is prophesying One who will crush the head of Moab—the same language as the snake-crusher in Genesis 3.15. Mention of a "sceptre" revisits Judah's promised sceptre from Genesis 49, a shepherd's staff become a king's token. A star will rise, he says. A shining star, followed by a mighty sceptre. After Moab, he goes on to speak of neighbouring Edom and Seir being dispossessed. Balaam, who came "from the east" (Num 23:7), is predicting an Israelite king who will demand the allegiance of all the peoples of the east.

This "star" would later come to be understood in Jewish tradition as speaking of the promised Messiah—one who would have great glory. In the Talmuds[7] and the Dead Sea Scrolls[8] the star is interpreted as being a messianic figure. Second-century Jewish rebel leader Simeon bar Kosiba had his surname changed to "bar Kokhba" (son of the Star) as a messianic designation.[9]

The secretaries pack up their clay tablets and chisels, and take them back to the libraries of Moab. This is a significant prophecy for them, because it announces one who will rule over them from Israel in the future. Generation after generation of wise men, astrologers, sorcerers and magi will pore over these tablets, will copy and store them—because they respect the words of Balaam, and because these words speak of a pending national doom. For centuries, men standing in the tradition of Balaam will interrogate the scrolls and the stars, searching for a sign that this promised one is near.

---

7. *Targum Jonathan* on Numbers 24:7.

8. *Damascus Document* 7:19–20.

9. Palestinian Talmud *Ta'anit* 68d.

MATTHEW'S MAGI

The magi of Matthew's gospel, according to the Fathers like Leo the Great, Cesarius of Arles and Eusebius, were the custodians of this tradition. They stood, centuries later, in the same academic school. Origen records this as a well-known tradition,

> It is said that from Balaam arose the caste and the institution of the Magi which had flourished in the East. They had in their possession in writing all that Balaam had prophesied, including "A star shall come forth from Jacob and a man shall rise from Israel." The Magi held these writings among themselves. Consequently when Jesus was born, they recognized the star and understood that the prophecy had come to fulfilment.[10]

They knew from their books, from the oracles attributed to Balaam, that "a star will rise out of Jacob" means the sceptre will follow, and the crushing of Moab. On seeing Christ's birth-star, why do they set out with gifts? To seek his patronage, to pre-empt his wrath. Gifts are gestures of reciprocity, tokens of friendship (Prov 18:16). Psalm 2, which mentions Messiah and the same staff/sceptre, warns surrounding kings to "Kiss the Son, lest he be angry." The wise men are responding to the warnings of Balaam's oracle. They have positioned themselves to take seriously their own prophet in a way that the people of Israel did not take seriously their own national prophets, as Cesarius of Arles complained accusingly:

> If God's prophecies were inserted in the sacred books by Moses, how much more so were they copied by men who then lived in Mesopotamia, for they considered Balaam splendid and certainly were disciples of his art! After his time the profession and instruction of the seers is said to have flourished in parts of the Orient. Possessing copies of everything which Balaam prophesied, they even have it written: "A star shall advance from Jacob, and a man shall rise from Israel." The magi kept these writings more among themselves, and so when Jesus was born they recognised the star and understood that the prophecy was fulfilled more than did the people of Israel who disdained to hear the words of the holy prophets. Therefore, only from the writings which Balaam had left, they learned that the time was approaching, came and immediately sought to adore him.[11]

10. Origen, *Homily in the Book of Numbers,* 13:7.
11. Cesarius of Arles, Sermon 113:2.

But here there is a problem. Were not Matthew's magi from Persia—modern Iran—not from Arabia? There is certainly a long tradition of their Persian origin, including an anecdote in which the invading Persian general, walking into Bethlehem's Church of the Nativity in 610 AD, saw a mosaic depicting the nativity, in which the wise men were dressed as Parthian priests. The Persians, moved that their own holy men would be so honoured in a far-off country, chose not to destroy the church.[12]

However, there is an even older witness to the wise men being from Arabia. Justin Martyr in AD160, wrote "The wise men from Arabia came to Bethlehem and worshipped the child and offered to him gifts, gold, frankincense and myrrh."[13] Tertullian and Clement of Rome also testify to the wise men being Arabian.[14] "From the east," Matthew's phrase, which mimics the phrase in the Balaam story, means, for those in Palestine, from the immediate east—the desert across the Jordan river that stretches endlessly down into the Arabian peninsula—modern Jordan and Saudi. Kenneth Bailey, interviewing people across the Holy Land, declares that "from the east" in everyday speech in Palestine always means from this region.[15]

Their gifts also speak of their origins. Traditionally, one brings gifts from one's homeland when one visits internationally. If I travel from the UK to somewhere else, I take shortbread in a tin with the Union Jack flag on its lid. If a Turkish friend visits, they invariably bring Turkish delight or baklava. My Pakistani friends give gifts of Pakistani clothes. If someone travels from their village to another village, they take their village's unique flavour of olives, or a local cheese, or a local style of handicraft. Gold comes from Sheba—Arabia. To be sure, other nations had gold, but it makes more sense as tribute from its land of origin. If this embassy of the magi depicts a nation responding to an ancient oracle about a rising star heralding their subjugation or annexation, and if these gifts are pre-emptive token of tribute, then gifts representing their internationally-identifiable profile are most natural. And, even more compellingly, frankincense and myrrh are harvested from trees that only grow in the Arabian peninsula. The magi are bringing the glory of their homeland to Jesus, their most prized local exports, flavours of their nation.[16]

---

12. Blincoe, *Bethlehem*, 110.

13. Justin Martyr, *Dialogue with Trypho*, 78.

14. Brown, *Birth of the Messiah*, 169–170.

15. Bailey, *Middle Eastern Eyes*, 52.

16. See Revelation 21:24.

ISAIAH 60

There is another ancient oracle that seems to have been in Matthew's thinking as he wrote of the wise men. There are definite resonances of Isaiah 60:1–7 in the Matthew 2 story.

> Arise, shine, for your light has come, and the glory of the LORD has risen upon you.
>
> For behold, darkness shall cover the earth, and thick darkness the peoples; but the LORD will arise upon you, and his glory will be seen upon you.
>
> And nations shall come to your light, and kings to the brightness of your rising.
>
> Lift up your eyes all around, and see; they all gather together, they come to you; your sons shall come from afar, and your daughters shall be carried on the hip.
>
> Then you shall see and be radiant; your heart shall thrill and exult, because the abundance of the sea shall be turned to you, the wealth of the nations shall come to you.
>
> A multitude of camels shall cover you, the young camels of Midian and Ephah; all those from Sheba shall come. They shall bring gold and frankincense, and shall bring good news, the praises of the LORD.
>
> All the flocks of Kedar shall be gathered to you; the rams of Nebaioth shall minister to you; they shall come up with acceptance on my altar, and I will beautify my beautiful house. Isaiah 60:1–7

Isaiah's prophecy was intended for Zion (Jerusalem), but fulfilled in the child of Bethlehem. He speaks of the rising of a great light. Nations (meaning Gentile, foreign, "outsider" nations), represented in the magi, come. "Camels" create an image of a caravan of Arabs coming up from the desert, and undoubtedly this is how the magi would have travelled. Explicitly, Isaiah prophesies the bringing of gold and frankincense. Matthew expands the gifts to include myrrh. He knows the end of the story that Isaiah could not know, and myrrh is the fragrance of death. Matthew, writing on the other side of the death and resurrection of Jesus Christ, reflects on the magi's prophetic insight to bring not only gold and frankincense, but also myrrh—the sweet-smelling spice used in burial to mask the odour of the dead—as a sign of Jesus' burial.

Matthew's readers, who knew Isaiah 60, would have expected the magi to bring gold and frankincense. Myrrh, though, would have been a surprise, an unexpected gift that would not have immediately made sense.

Why would you give a new-born baby a token of death? Why would you present a king whom you were trying to placate a reminder of his mortality? Such things are not done! Yet here, as Word becomes flesh, as immortal becomes mortal, such a note is utterly and perfectly appropriate. Mortality takes the national triumphalism out of Isaiah 60. And Jesus' eternal kingdom is only achieved through his burial, and only entered through our burial, at baptism. And Bethlehem? Bethlehem has always been a place where the Beloved dies.

Verse seven speaks of flocks of sheep belonging to nomadic shepherd-tribes in the desert being brought up to be sacrificed on the Jerusalem altar. All of these are seen as signs of "the nations" bringing tribute to Israel's God. Such a danger here of ethnocentric arrogance—"they" are coming to "our" temple, to "our" God. So much injustice can arise from mistakenly aligning one's national narrative with the purposes of God!

And here is the wisdom of God. That this prophecy is fulfilled, not in the physical city of Jerusalem, not in Solomon's or Herod's mighty temple edifice, but in the Child. The magi arrive at Jerusalem, only to be re-directed to Bethlehem. This re-directing must happen to us all at some point. Jesus is the new Jerusalem. He is the new centre. Bailey, after his thorough exegesis of Isaiah 60, arrives at this stunning conclusion.

> Although the glorious events projected for honouring the city of Jerusalem never happened, the Gospel authors perceived them to be taking place in the birth of Jesus. Around the *child* there was a great light and the glory of the Lord appeared. To the *child* came Arab wise men from the desert on camels bringing gold and frankincense. Shepherds visited the *child,* not the city. The great hopes for the city were transferred to the child in a manger. Indeed, "the glory of the Lord shone round about" the *child.* This shift from the city to the child is significant. The birth stories "de-Zionize" the tradition.[17]

The locus of prophetic fulfilment moves from a place to a person, from Jerusalem to Jesus, from the palace to the periphery. The magi are mistaken and re-directed. This truth is of enormous significance for Christianity. Our faith, unlike the other great ancient religions, does not have a geographic centre. By implication, there is no holy city, holy land, special ethnicity or sacred language. Or, more precisely, the sacredness of the "land" is now expanded to the whole earth. All land is sacred. All languages are redeemed.

17. Bailey, *Middle Eastern Eyes,* 54.

All ethnic groups are included on equal footing. The concept of "land" is maximised, rather than minimised,[18] as Palestinian theologian Salim Munayer writes, "The blessing of the Promised Land has been stretched over the whole earth, stretched far but not thin. The whole earth is filled with promise."[19]

If the Balaam verses provided the outline, speaking of a rising star, Isaiah 60, also speaking of a light which rises, colours in more detail. Finally, even more colour is added by Psalm 72:10–11.

> May the kings of Tarshish and of the coastlands render him tribute; may the kings of Sheba and Seba bring gifts!
> May all kings fall down before him, all nations serve him!
> Psalm 72:1–11

In this verse we have the combination of tribute, Sheba and Seba (Arabia), all nations, and kings "falling down"—the same phrase used by Matthew as the magi "fell down and worshipped" in Matthew 2:11. It is from these verses in the background of Matthew 2 (Is 60 and Ps 72), that the magi came to be thought of as kings in their own right (hence the Christmas carol "We Three Kings"), although this fulfilment could just as easily have been by proxy, with the magi as royal ambassadors. The idea, in the carol and the tradition, that there were *three* wise men/kings, arises from the fact that Matthew mentions three gifts, and also from the Balaam story. Balaam had two servants with him—they were three (Num 22:22).[20]

Balak, the wicked king and enemy of God's people, employed a foreign Magus to destroy his enemy, but in an unexpected twist this magus from the desert, Balaam, honoured and blessed them. Centuries later Herod, the wicked king and enemy of God's people, sought to employ these foreign magi from the east so he could destroy God's anointed, but instead they blessed and honoured the Christ child.[21]

---

18. One example from Paul is Ephesians 6:2–3 where, quoting from Exodus 20:12, Paul takes a promise regarding the "land" and presents it as regarding the whole earth.

19. Munayer, "Theology of the Land," 251.

20. Brown, *Birth of the Messiah*, 193.

21. There is also a midrashic Pharaoh-like characterisation of Herod. The popular story in the first century was that Pharaoh and his evil sorcerer advisors sought to destroy Moses at birth, and ended up killing all the Hebrew children. There are clear resonances of this in the Jesus story. As divine punishment, Pharaoh, who drowned Hebrew babies in the Nile, has the Nile turned to blood, and is eventually himself drowned.

There are multiple significances of the Balaam prophecy. It is important that non-Jewish characters are part of the Bethlehem story. Bethlehem, on the edge of the desert, with a Jewish and an Arabic name, welcomes the magi from the east. Ruth the Moabitess will come up from the east to receive the hospitality of the House of Bread. At the birth of Jesus, a star comes out of Jacob, and a sceptre rises in Israel. A king for all nations is born. The Seed who will crush the head of the Snake arises in the last days. The child of Bethlehem is king of the world.

5

Rahab
Enemy to Family

But Rahab the prostitute and her father's household and all who belonged to her, Joshua saved alive. And she has lived in Israel to this day, because she hid the messengers whom Joshua sent to spy out Jericho.

—JOSHUA 6:25

JERICHO. ONE OF THE oldest cities in the world. City of palms, where the Judean wilderness meets the Jordan valley, and date palms stretch as far as the eye can see. It's harvest time, early spring, when the river flows at its fullest and the first sheaves of barley are gathered.[1] God's people cross the Jordan from east to west—in Scripture, journeying eastwards is always exile and westwards is always homecoming. The manna from heaven is switched off immediately they enter the Land—the land itself will feed them now.

The account of the conquest of the city is stacked with the number seven—God's number.[2] The city falls on the sabbath when man cannot

---

1. Thompson, *The Land and the Book,* 1: 362–363.
2. E.g. Joshua 6:4, 13, 15.

work. The whole point is that it is God's victory—God gives them rest. "The bizarre strategy confirmed that Israel could not attribute victory to its own military prowess. Their victory was a gift of grace—an astounding work of the Lord."[3]

The entire city wall collapses to the ground—except for one house. The one earthquake-proof house in the city wall. Rahab's house. The whole city is burned with fire, except for one house. The one fire-proof house in all Jericho. Rahab's house. The door opens, and out into the fire-blackened remains of their former life stumble Rahab, her parents, her brothers, and all the other relatives who had squeezed in along with her.

Rahab the prostitute lived in the city wall. Houses in the city wall are the most vulnerable to enemy attack—the king lives in the centre, which is safest. She was, both architecturally and socially, marginal. Yet we know her name, while the king of Jericho remains unnamed. Scripture, in Testaments both old and new, honours Rahab. In fact, Rahab's high-shame social marginalisation could well be why she was prepared to gamble on the Israelite invasion as a route to a better life. Dissatisfaction leads to action. Gottwald puts it like this:

> Rahab's susceptibility to participating in a conspiracy to overthrow the city's ruling class is understandable when we note that in the typical ancient city harlots formed one of several groups of occupational outcasts whose services were greatly desired but who, because of their demeaning work and the social taboos, codes, and conventions which they breached, bore a scapegoating stigma and worked under decided disabilities.[4]

Rahab's faith, praised in Hebrews 11:31 and James 2:25, is faith expressed in hospitality, and hospitality in its broadest sense; the welcome of strangers, the love of enemies. The two spies on their scouting expedition are received, hidden, and protected by Rahab. To welcome God's people is to welcome God, and hospitality in Scripture never goes unrewarded.

There is a note of the Exodus in Rahab's action. A relatively rare word for "hide" (*tspn*) is used when she conceals the two Israelites, the same word used when Moses' mother hid him. Rahab is like the midwives who directly disobey the king's command. Women in both stories save men.

We can also hear a note of the Sodom story from Genesis 19. Both stories take place in the Jordan valley, both are about non-hospitable cities

3. Schreiner, *The King in his Beauty*, 100.
4. Gottwald, *Tribes*, 557.

failing to receive two messengers from God, and both cities are destroyed. In both stories, the host is a marginal person whose honourable action despite their shameful social location renders the city even more culpable. In both stories, a demand to "bring out the men" is defied, and "escape to the hills" is the result. Both hosts are named, saved, and produce offspring who are also named.

Rahab uses an important word, *khesed,* to articulate how she expects her hospitality to initiate a relationship between her and the people of God. *Khesed,* which is often translated loving kindness, is a term rich with Middle Eastern relational overtones of mutuality, reciprocity and loyalty. Exchange of gifts or favours forges a relationship. Mutual expectations of allegiance grow and are strengthened into an informal covenant or arrangement by which both parties are tied to each other by a bond of honour, gratitude and interdependence. This is what Rahab is expecting when she says:

> Now then, please swear to me by the LORD that, as I have dealt kindly with you (*khesed*), you also will deal kindly (*khesed*) with my father's house, and give me a sure sign that you will save alive my father and mother, my brothers and sisters, and all who belong to them, and deliver our lives from death." Joshua 2:12–13

Bultmann explains it like this:

> In the OT *khesed* denotes an attitude of man or God which arises out of a mutual relationship. It is the attitude which the one expects of the other in this relationship, and to which he is pledged in relation to him.[5]

According to Zeba Crook, "the central meaning of *khesed* implies a relationship of mutual obligation."[6] This can be a symmetrical exchange between peers, or an asymmetrical exchange, between a powerful patron or benefactor, and a dependent client, in which instance the patron is responsible for protection and generosity, and the client for fealty and gratitude. Rahab expects, and receives, a reciprocation of her hospitality.

At their word, Rahab invites all of her relatives into her house, inviting them to trust her prediction that destruction is coming, and that only those who enter will be saved. She hangs a red cord from the window in the wall, reminding us of the lamb's blood at Passover, and of the red cord in the story of another marginal woman, Tamar, forcing her way into the

---

5. Bultmann, "ελεος," 2:479.
6. Crook, "Reciprocity," 87.

messianic line. "The scarlet cord," writes Tikva Frymer-Kensky, "brings Rahab into the august company of the barrier-breakers of David's ancestry."[7]

Rahab's house is like Noah's ark. Those who enter are saved, those who don't are destroyed. Those who are saved tumble out into a new world. In this, Rahab's house is like Jesus' house. Those who enter are saved, those who don't are destroyed. Rahab goes from being enemy to family. She transitions from shame to honour. She is marginal in Jericho's story but central to the genealogy of Messiah. She escapes a city earmarked for destruction and relocates to a village earmarked for destiny.

As we gaze at Rahab, we catch a glimpse of her descendant Jesus. Jesus was despised and marginal. He risked his life to save us. His house is the only one that is proof against the eschatological earthquake. Those who enter are saved. Those who refuse will not survive. It's three thousand five hundred years earlier, yet when we look at the face of Rahab, we see something of Jesus!

And then our story takes a breath-taking turn. Rahab, the refugee prostitute with her whole family in tow, carrying everything they own, marries a prince! Salmon was one of the leading men of Judah. His father, Nahshon, was the chief of his ancestral tribe, the royal tribe of Judah. When Moses chose one man to represent each tribe, Nahshon stood on Judah's behalf (Num 1:4–7, 16). In 1 Chronicles 2:10, Nahshon is called "prince of the sons of Judah." Nahshon's son Salmon is called by the chronicler, "the father of Bethlehem" (1 Chr 2:51). It seems that at some point after the fall of Jericho, while Israel was travelling about taking her inheritance, Salmon married Rahab. And when Judah received her allotted lands in the south of the country, Salmon took Rahab up the hill to set up home in Bethlehem. And they had a son. His name was Boaz.

Salmon's offer of marriage to Rahab is remarkable for several reasons. Highborn shouldn't marry lowborn—not in the stratified society of the East. Insider shouldn't marry outsider—especially not an enemy, a pagan from a polytheistic race, a Canaanite. And also, it's not as if Salmon's family were settled and established with capacity to spare to welcome Rahab and her family into their mix. They were themselves just limping out of the desert, bedraggled and exhausted. Surely Salmon was eligible for the age-old exemption from generosity, "charity begins at home. Let us sort ourselves out first and then we can think about helping others." Yet here we see this under-celebrated hero taking his place in the messianic ancestry.

7. Frymer-Kensky, *Women of the Bible*, 39.

Matthew shows us in his genealogy how the family tree fits together:

> . . . and Ram the father of Amminadab, and Amminadab the father
> of Nahshon, and Nahshon the father of Salmon, and Salmon the
> father of Boaz by Rahab, and Boaz the father of Obed by Ruth, and
> Obed the father of Jesse, and Jesse the father of David the king.
> Matthew 1:4–6

The chronology that gets us from Salmon to David can be problematic but not insurmountable. The time from conquest to monarchy should include a few more links in the chain. Probably, there were a few unremarkable Judahites between Salmon and Boaz. However, the Rabbis were very happy to preserve this genealogy, and if we are able to lay chronological concerns to one side for a moment, we see that Rahab, like Tamar before her and Ruth after her, is rewarded by both Old Testament narrators and Matthew, with a place in the story of the Messiah.

For Palestinian Christians, Joshua 6 raises difficult questions about Israel, about *herem* ("the ban" – the devoting of people to destruction, as in 6:17), about Old Testament hermeneutics. If read outside of its salvation-historical context, the book of Joshua can be seen to justify atrocities in the name of Zionism, as though Israelis had divine sanction to take Palestinian lives. Munther Isaac shows a way through for this difficult text, which pivots on the inclusion of Rahab among the people of God.

> Is it not amazing that a Gentile woman and prostitute is the hero of
> this story? Is it not amazing that Rahab found her way into the ge-
> nealogy of Jesus? Who said that the God of the OT is the God of the
> Jews alone? Who said that the God of the OT is an exclusive God?[8]

Rahab's hospitality qualifies her to be part of the fabric, even the foundations, of Bethlehem, house of divine hospitality. Because she showed *khesed* to vulnerable outsiders, Rahab, as a refugee, is welcomed by the *khesed* of God, through Salmon, into Bethlehem, which will shelter many more refugees as the story unfolds. Rahab, as a marginal character, makes her home here in the place where unlikely heroes preponderate, and where vulnerability is part of the fabric of life.

> Rahab's name means "wide, broad." She is the "broad of Jericho."
> Her name is emblematic of the permeable boundaries of Israel. She
> is the wide-open woman who is the wide-open door to Canaan, or
> maybe (in the negative view) the wide-open door to apostasy. To

8. Isaac, "Reading the Old Testament," 231.

[some], open boundaries are dangerous; others can see them as presenting an opportunity.[9]

Other than Rahab, there is only one other well-developed character in the first half of Joshua. His name is Achan, and he is the direct opposite of Rahab. As so often in Scripture, we are shown two examples, one honourable, one shameful. As readers, we are encouraged to compare the two characters and draw our own conclusions.

Achan is on the other side during the battle for Jericho. He is from the tribe of Judah. He seems to have been fairly wealthy—he owned a great deal of portable wealth in livestock (Josh 7:24). His name means "troubler."[10] For his sin of covetousness (Josh 7:21), a direct breach of the tenth commandment, he and his entire household are placed under "the ban" that is reserved for the enemies of God. They are stoned with stones and burned with fire.

Achan's story, in Joshua 7, is a thorough juxtaposition of Rahab's story. He is male, she is female. He is a privileged insider of Judahite pedigree, yet he disqualifies himself and comes under "the ban."[11] Rahab is a "banned" outsider, yet she becomes an insider—being joined to Judah, the tribe forfeited by Achan. Rahab and her whole family are brought in, whilst Achan and his whole family are cast out. Rahab received reciprocal *khesed* for the *khesed* she had shown to Israel, whilst Achan received *achar* (trouble) for the *achar* which he had brought on Israel (Josh 7:25). The legacy of both is said to last "to this day." The contrast between Rahab and Achan is displayed below.

Rahab	Achan
Canaanite woman	Jewish man
Prostitute	Impeccable pedigree (Judah, no less!)
Hesed reciprocated	*Achar* reciprocated
Saved from the ban along with family	Comes under the ban along with family
Shame to honour	Honour to shame
Outsider to insider	Insider to outsider
Added to Judah	Removed from Judah
Lives in Israel "to this day" (6:25)	Mound of stones "to this day" (7:26)

Contrast between Rahab and Achan

9. Frymer-Kensky, *Women of the Bible*, 44.

10. His name Achan, the word "trouble," and the place where he is executed, Achor, share the same root.

11. Moberley, *Old Testament Theology*, Kindle Location 1867.

Rahab is the first recorded refugee to find a new home in Bethlehem, but by no means the last. She was soon followed by her future daughter-in-law Ruth, after whom Bethlehem would be the House of Bread to many generations of refugees. This story of hospitality to refugees continues until as recently as 1915, when 100 Armenian and Syriac Christian families fleeing persecution in Turkey found shelter in Bethlehem, and 1948, when three camps of dispossessed Palestinians sprang up in the Bethlehem area—camps which are still there today. This 1948 influx of refugees nearly quadrupled the population from 9,000 to 35,000 almost overnight.[12] The largest of these camps is Dheishah, meaning *A Splendour of Greenery*, because the site—a former quarry—was now filled with lush trees, and had been a favourite leisure spot for locals before becoming a home for those fleeing during the *Nakba* (when many Palestinians were forcibly expelled from their ancestral homes).[13]

This great tradition of refugees being assimilated into Bethlehem life, which started with Rahab, is something modern Bethlehemites are proud of. In February 2017, Yaqub Shaheen won *Arab Idol,* an extremely popular talent show. Yaqub is from a Bethlehemite Syriac family. The Syriacs, or Suriani, are an ancient Christian sect who still worship every Sunday in Aramaic, the language of Christ.[14] Fleeing Turkey in 1915, the Syriacs were subsumed into Bethlehem life, and they live there, as the biblical author said of Rahab, "to this day."

Joshua seems to be one of the Old Testament books most mis-used by those who feel election is ethnic, and those who in the name of God have stolen lands and subjugated others, justified apartheids and genocides. The Rahab story is a huge antidote to such abuses. This story is our story, we were shame-filled enemies who were brought near and included in Christ. We see another mighty mother in Jesus' genealogy, Bethlehem welcoming another refugee, a sacrificial shame-remover in Salmon, and the family of God swelling joyfully with outsiders brought in.

12. River, *Bethlehem,* Kindle Location 719.

13. Raheb & Strickert, *Bethlehem 2000,* 138.

14. Blincoe, *Bethlehem,* 108.

6

Ibzan
Bethlehem as a Thin Place

After him Ibzan of Bethlehem judged Israel.

He had thirty sons, and thirty daughters he gave in marriage outside his clan, and thirty daughters he brought in from outside for his sons. And he judged Israel seven years.

Then Ibzan died and was buried at Bethlehem.

—JUDGES 12:8–10

UP THE HILL TO Bethlehem come thirty young brides-to-be, all daughters of leading families from the surrounding clans, all coming to make their homes in Bethlehem. Bethlehem is liminal space. An inter-zone. A border town. It is an airlock between the cultivated and the desert, civilisation and chaos. It has both a Hebrew and an Arabic name. It is a soft margin. Looking west from Bethlehem, one sees Jerusalem, order, urbanity, civilisation. Looking east, there is wilderness with its ancient expanses of unpredictability, rawness and ferocity.

There is a tendency, there has always been a tendency, for people to draw hard lines around their identity. Us-them. Insider-outsider. Clean-unclean. Good-bad. Many cultures through the ages have viewed outsiders as barbarian, as a threat to order. Ethnic purity is seen as good, mixing as evil. Fear reigns.

The story of Bethlehem is different. Bethlehem has always been, and still is, a place of diversity. The genealogy of Jesus makes this clear, with Matthew the Evangelist drawing attention to outsiders brought in, to Tamar and Rahab and Ruth and Bathsheba. Boaz' mother was Canaanite, Obed's mother was Moabite, Solomon's mother was probably Hittite, and Rehoboam's mother was Ammonite. These are not shameful anomalies in Jesus' otherwise pure Jewish DNA, to be swept under the carpet. Matthew seems to miss other individuals out, he could easily have skipped these outsiders too, were he ashamed of them! On the contrary, they are a sign that Messiah came for all people. Matthew, writing for a Jewish audience, seeks to emphasise this right at the start of his gospel. These names are a celebration of diversity. There is a reason Jesus was not born in a xenophobic, right wing Levite city. Narratives of ethnic purity smack of fascism. Embrace of "the other" is fundamental to the story of Messiah.

One of the minor judges, who is only given three verses, exemplifies this Bethlehemite culture of intentional openness to "the other." All we know about Ibzan is that he was born and died in Bethlehem,[1] that he was extremely fertile, and that he understood the benefits of exogamy— of marriage with "outsiders." Marriage was for alliance, and we see Ibzan as a shrewd political actor, marrying his sons to thirty foreign girls, and marrying his daughters to thirty foreign guys. Given Bethlehem's exposure and vulnerability, and the perennial proximity of enemy tribes, it was great wisdom for Ibzan to bind his enemies to himself through cords of kinship. Kinship by marriage is sacred in the Near East, and marriage alliances prove powerful protection.

This policy does seem to contradict the warnings against marrying foreigners in other parts of the Old Testament. Whatever prohibitions like those in Deuteronomy 7:2–4 mean, they cannot be grounds for racism. They cannot constitute a justification for discrimination against people on

---

1. Some scholars propose that Ibzan was from a northern Bethlehem in Zebulun and not Bethlehem in Judah. However, as yet no archaeological evidence for an Iron Age northern Bethlehem, mentioned only in Joshua 19:15, has been discovered. Butler, *Judges*, 297.

grounds of ethnicity. So what are we to do with the many accounts of "outsider marriage" in the Bible? According to Frymer-Kensky:

> The many stories about marriage to outsiders dramatize the boundary issues that marriage presents. Marriage is always a threshold action . . . Marriage is fraught with the danger of change, and this danger is at the heart of the dispute over non-Israelite women . . . The biblical stories about marriages to outside women and their consequences were the natural vehicle with which Israel expressed and explored the dimensions of this perennial issue.[2]

Without going into a full discussion of this complex issue, a few comments are in order here. Firstly, these prohibitions are embedded in an ancient Near Eastern culture in which outsiderness was typically associated with deviant morality.[3] This idea is mirrored in the English word "outlandish," which, though technically referring to where people are from, also implies inappropriate or strange behaviour. Secondly, the people of Israel at the time of the conquest were in the minority, and the surrounding peoples were "more numerous" and "mightier" (Deut 7:1). So there is a power-differential at work; Israel as a tiny, bedraggled minority surrounded by powerful, sophisticated nations protecting herself is very different to a powerful majority using such verses to claim divine approval for their oppression of the minorities entrusted to their care. When vulnerability is discounted, the Scripture is twisted beyond recognition. Thirdly, we Christians stand removed from these verses by culture, millennia and ultimately by covenant; the New Covenant in Christ overcomes all ethnic divisions, and discrimination on the basis of nationality finds no New Testament backing whatsoever.

These prohibitions were never about ethnic purity. Indeed, there is a lot in the Old Testament about the rights of outsiders who dwell among Israel. They were about spiritual purity, and the risk therewith. To mis-evaluate such prohibitions without taking account of the wider perspective of Scripture is to set a dangerous interpretive trajectory that leads ultimately to the very attitudes prevalent in Israel which Jesus spent so much time confronting; ethnocentrism, superiority, prejudice, otherization, attitudes which today are the great enemy of the inclusive mission of God, as Volf

---

2. Frymer-Kensky, *Women of the Bible*, 334.

3. Walton and Walton, *The Lost World*, 152.

has sagely written, "religion must be de-ethnicized so that ethnicity can be de-sacralized."[4]

Many commentators criticise Ibzan for the very thing we are celebrating, yet the writer of Judges makes no moral evaluation, either good or bad, he simply relates the facts. Indeed, seven is God's number, the number of completeness, so it could be argued that Ibzan's period of leadership is shown here to be godly.

There is a midrash which identifies Ibzan as Boaz.[5] This is a common Midrashic technique, identifying a major biblical character as a minor one in order to flesh out the character a little.[6] Although there is insufficient evidence to support this claim, other than them both being from noble families in Bethlehem during the time of the Judges, and sharing b-z in the root of their names, this tradition adds some interesting colour to the Boaz story. That the Rabbis generally viewed Ibzan in a positive light is instructive. If it were true that Boaz had so many children, then he didn't *need* to marry Ruth for his own continuity, so it emphasises his compassion and condescension in doing so. Also, it would show that he was amenable to outsiders, laying the groundwork for his acceptance of Ruth.[7]

Where a major part of the social disintegration demonstrated in the book of Judges is otherisation, rejection of and violence towards "the other" because of their ethnicity or status or history or gender, the story of Boaz and Ruth is a corrective to this attitude, a story of the hospitality of God and the humanisation of the outsider.

The evidence that Ibzan is Boaz is insufficient. But I do think that Ibzan reinforces our understanding of Bethlehem's unique role within otherwise mostly ethno-exclusive Israel as a place of acceptance, a semi-porous membrane through which outsiders are assimilated into the people of God. Raheb and Strickert write:

> During this early period of history, one of the central characteristics of Bethlehem was its mixed population and mutual tolerance among people of different ethnic, religious and cultural backgrounds. . . . One of the famous judges of Israel was a man from

4. Volf, *Exclusion and Embrace*, 49.

5. Bava Batra 91a, cited in Rashi (1:1).

6. A technique colloquially known as "conservation of biblical personalities." Ziegler, *Ruth*, 90.

7. Ziegler, *Ruth*, 91.

Bethlehem called Ibzan, who was known for encouraging his own children to be open to such intermarriage.[8]

There is something wonderfully playing-field-levelling about the fact that Ibzan gave daughters away to "the outside" and brought in wives for his sons from "the outside." This give and take across cultural divides is the best way to approach cultural difference. There is always something to learn and something to teach, something to contribute and something to receive. Keeping the flow of giving and receiving as two-way traffic rescues both sides from ethnic pride in its various guises. As Niles, the Sri Lankan theologian wrote, "The only way to build love between two people or two groups of people is to be so related to each other as to stand in need of each other. The Christian community must serve. It must also be in a position where it needs to be served."[9]

Bailey, reflecting Niles, writes, "We in the West go with our technology, which often is the point of our greatest strength and often reflects the developing world's greatest weakness. This tends to stimulate pride in the giver and humiliation in the receiver."[10] The way to break this cycle of pride and humiliation, to level, as much as possible, the ground between both parties, is to do what Ibzan, this anti-racist pioneer, learned long ago, to make sure that there is equal measure in this grace of giving and receiving.

Sons and daughters of Bethlehem, xenophobia is not an option for us! It is contrary to our heritage in Jesus. As Jesus' ancestry was filled with outsiders-brought-in, so should our churches be. As Ibzan was both a giver and receiver across cultural divides, so should we be. Instead of fear, embrace. Instead of reluctance, hospitality. Instead of mono-culture, multi-culture.

In a world where so much trouble arises at ethnic fault lines, how appropriate for the Prince of Peace to appear in the town of Ibzan. Jesus, Son of God and Son of Man, born according to God's purposes in the liminal space, between garden and wilderness, the Reconciler!

Bethlehem's geography, today as three and half thousand years ago, is rich with metaphor. Bethlehem is open to the eastern and the western horizons, as is the religion that was born on its hills. Neither East nor West can claim exclusive rights over Christ. Both kneel before the manger. Blincoe,

---

8. Raheb & Strickert, *Bethlehem 2000*, 22.

9. Niles, *This Jesus*, 23–27.

10. Bailey, *Middle Eastern Eyes*, 204.

a British historian married to Palestinian film-maker Leila Sansour, puts it like this:

> This is Bethlehem: an old town facing the site of an even older town, sitting at the edge of the desert, just six miles south of Jerusalem. Throughout all its cat's lives, Bethlehem has been defined by this position. The desert is the home to the Bedouin and the pathway to an ancient world of nomads and caravans, shepherds and Magi, and the great, lost civilizations of the Middle East. Jerusalem is the gate to the west, an open door that too easily gives way to occupiers and invaders. Today, it is the road into Israel, described in the language of the 1949 Geneva Convention as the "hostile occupying power." Bethlehem is caught between its past and present; its face turned to the desert as though stretching out for warmth or perhaps hoping for a new day.[11]

Early Christians built their monasteries in the liminal space all around Bethlehem, hovering like mirages on the edge of the desert. Many of these very old monasteries can still be visited today. Centuries later, this idea was carried by the Celtic Christians to the islands of Britain, expressing their belief that God was to be found in the "thin" places, on the thresholds of the world. Early British Christians would leave their legacy in outlying coastal areas for the same reason, in desolate, wind-swept Lindisfarne and Iona. God, they said, dwells where the edge is. He is most present, they preached, in the margins. I wonder, as I gaze out over the desert, what do we miss today with the widespread narrative of having to be in the centres of power? Christ wasn't born amongst the Jerusalem elite, he was killed by them.

The Judean wilderness, stretching away eastwards from Bethlehem down to the Jordan Valley and, further south, to the Dead Sea, the lowest point on Earth, is a real desert. It's where John the Baptist positioned himself, calling people out of the towns and cities into the wild as a demonstration of their repentance. Repentance so often is a call to simplify, to get away from the complexities of urban life and into the austerity of the desert. It's where Jesus, who had something of the desert in his DNA and in his soul, spent his forty-day fast, de-toxifying and de-cluttering his soul in preparation for three arduous years of ministry. The romance of the desert has always attracted pilgrims, indeed Bethlehem's early Christian years were boosted by monastery-building as God-seekers fled their cities and sought new life in the wide-open spaces. Some of the monasteries in the

---

11. Blincoe, *Bethlehem*, 21.

Bethlehem area are incredible! Dalrymple, interviewing a contemporary desert monk, captured a hauntingly beautiful articulation of this human desire for simplicity.

> "God is everywhere, so you can find him everywhere." He gestured to the darkening sand dunes outside: "But in the desert, in the pure, clean atmosphere, in the silence—there you can find *yourself*. And unless you begin to know yourself, how can you even begin to search for God?"[12]

Of course, most people on the planet today live in cities. The vast majority of us do not have the luxury of going on a desert pilgrimage. And yet, this principle remains. God is present in the margins, and our cities are full of marginalised people. Bethlehem can be found in the city now, in a Mumbai slum, an Istanbul *gecekondu*, a Sao Paulo *favela*. Mission at the margins of the world does not have to be in a lonely village – the urban poor are just as much a "thin" place, just as overlooked and disenfranchised and in need of a Saviour. If you like, the geographic "edge" in which Bethlehem is situated corresponds to a demographic, social, political "edge" in today's world. And the edge is where Jesus is present.

---

12. Dalrymple, *From the Holy Mountain*, 410.

7

The Concubine
Hospitality and Hatred

And all who saw it said, "Such a thing has never happened or been seen
from the day that the people of Israel came up out of the land of Egypt until
this day; consider it, take counsel, and speak."

—JUDGES 19:30

THE DARK DAYS OF the final chapters of Judges tell a nauseating tale of
gang rape, murder and bloody vengeance. These are difficult chapters, a
low point in the story. How is the reader to find a way in, to find purchase
in these accounts? Well, these chapters are replete with place names. The
author keeps pointing out *where* these things are taking place. That is a key
indicator—the most significant thing about these events is their geography.

Judges 19–21 paints the starkest of contrasts between Bethlehem in
Judah and Gibeah in Benjamin. When we get to the books of Samuel, we
will meet two rival kings, David of Bethlehem and Saul of Gibeah. These
stories are not only part of the apologetic for monarchy—"the nation is a
mess under the judges, and you really need a king." They are an apologetic
for David and *against* Saul. *For* Bethlehem and *against* Gibeah. They are

part of the story of Judah emerging and Benjamin decaying, part of the fulfilment of Rachel's deathbed prophecy.

But first, in Judges 19, we meet a woman from Bethlehem, who was living with a Levite from the north as a second-class wife or concubine. She has returned to her father's house in their ancestral village, staying for four months. We don't know why. We are told that she was unfaithful, but perhaps the return to her father's house was what was classed as unfaithfulness.[1] In due course, up the hill to Bethlehem comes the Levite, to find his woman and bring her home. The lady's father welcomes the Levite, and showers him with exemplary Middle Eastern hospitality. He is probably not wealthy (or else he would have been able to give his daughter with a dowry as a full wife), yet the author shows us in detail how he prevails on his guest to stay another day, and then another day. When he finally sends them on their way, he supplies them with more bread (*lehem*) (19:19). Bethlehem, ever the house of bread, here behaves honourably once again in welcoming those from outside.

Syrian commentator Abraham Mitrie Rihbany writes that these verses remind him of his village in Syria:

> His words are so much like those I often heard spoken in Syria on such occasions that it makes me feel homesick to read them. The ancient Bethlehemite was entertaining his son-in-law, who had stayed with them three days, the traditional length of such a visit in the East.[2]

In the Bible, as in many cultures today, hospitality is an index of godliness, and this son of Bethlehem demonstrates superb, extravagant hospitality towards an outsider. Bethlehem, House of Bread, is always open. Bread, considered sacred, must be shared. Rihbany, again, writes, "The *'aish* [bread] was something more than mere matter. Inasmuch as it sustained life, it was God's own life made tangible for his child, man, to feed upon."[3]

When the Levite and the woman finally set out on their homeward journey together, they must stop somewhere overnight on the way

---

1. Cheryl Exum has a good discussion on this chapter, confirming the view that *zanah* is not necessarily sexual unfaithfulness. "Originally the verb referred to an act related to a particular type of marriage, specifically to the woman's breach of patrilocal marriage to live with her husband: 'The unfaithfulness—to the father, to the old institution—for the sake of marriage, hence for sex, becomes [through linguistic development] sexual unfaithfulness.'" Exum, *Fragmented Women*, Kindle Location 3770.

2. Rihbany, *The Syrian Christ*, 156.

3. Rihbany, *The Syrian Christ*, 139.

northwards. Rather than stopping in Jerusalem, which at that time was still a Jebusite stronghold, they decide to stop in Gibeah, a small town in the territory of Benjamin. The man's logic is shown to us by the narrator:

> We will not turn aside into the city of foreigners, who do not belong to the people of Israel, but we will pass on to Gibeah." Judges 19:12

The widespread, natural suspicion of foreigners is in play here. "We are more likely to be well-treated by our own people than by foreigners," they say to themselves. Sadly, and ironically, Gibeah is shown to be the complete contrast of Bethlehem. Where Bethlehem was a place of hospitality, in Gibeah they sit in the square, long after dark, waiting for someone to welcome them into their home, according to custom, but they are ignored. No-one welcomes them in. Where Bethlehem is open to outsiders, hospitable, warm, Gibeah is cold, unwelcoming, uncaring. This neglect is shameful. "The person who fails to extend such hospitality brings reproach, not only upon himself, but upon his own clan and town."[4]

Finally, a foreigner who lives in Gibeah, who actually hails from the Ephraim hills—the same place as the Levite—welcomes them in as night is falling. During the night, the local Benjamites knock on the door and demand that the visitor be given over to them so that they can rape him. Why would they do this? Because they are antagonistic towards outsiders. They want to show any foreigner who is boss by dominating them, making them feel second-class, making it clear that they are not welcome. It bears reinforcing that rape is never about sexual desire. It is a weapon. It is a statement. It is an act of subjugation.

> "Let us know him" may indeed mean carnal knowledge, but the proposed rape of the traveller is like the rape of newcomers in jail. The purpose of such a rape is neither enjoyment nor love; it is the assertion of dominance and the dishonouring of the man forced to submit. Sexuality is often tied to power. Rape is violently attached to power, and male rape no less so.[5]

Exum makes a similar point: "Rape is a crime of violence not of passion; homosexual rape forces the male victim into a passive role, into the

---

4. Rihbany, *The Syrian Christ*, 146.
5. Frymer-Kensky, *Women of the Bible*, 124.

woman's position. The men of Gibeah want to humiliate the Levite in the most degrading way."[6]

This desire of the village men to humiliate the foreigner moves beyond neglect of the duty of hospitality into the domain of active anti-hospitality. If neglect is shameful, anti-hospitality is evil. It involves deliberate action to intimidate, humiliate or harm an outsider sufficiently to both punish and deter future incursion. It is the ultimate expression of xenophobia. Racist attacks, lynchings, pogroms, the Holocaust, and highly restrictive immigration policies are all manifestations of anti-hospitality.

In the Bible, as in this story, stories of hospitality and anti-hospitality are often placed side by side in order to create an honour-shame juxtaposition. For example, Genesis 18 shows Abraham's exemplary hospitality to the divine visitors, and Genesis 19, the proto-typical Sodom anti-hospitality narrative.[7] In the New Testament, gospel messengers frequently experience both hospitality and anti-hospitality. In Philippi, Paul and Silas encounter the hospitality of Lydia and of the Philippian jailor, but sandwiched between them the anti-hospitality of a racist attack in the marketplace, because they are Jews (Acts 16:11–40). So in this chapter, Bethlehem is the locus of honourable hospitality, Gibeah the home of shameful anti-hospitality.

The textual overlaps between this story and the Sodom story in Genesis 19 are numerous. In both instances two visitors wait in the town square, an outsider welcomes them where the locals will not, the men of the place come at night, surround the house, and demand that the guests be given over to them, and the suggestion is made that, instead of the guests, innocent young women should instead be handed over. Contrary to popular belief, the reason Sodom was destroyed was not for the sin of homosexuality, but for the sin of anti-hospitality. Ezekiel 16:49 makes this point, as Krish Kandiah explains,

> When the sin of Sodom is described by the prophet Ezekiel, he states, "Now this was the sin of your sister Sodom: she and her daughters were arrogant, overfed and unconcerned; they did not help the poor and needy. They were haughty and did detestable things before me." Passivity towards the poor and mistreatment of

---

6. Exum, *Fragmented Women*, Kindle Location 3826.

7. Matthews, *Cultural World*, 43.

the needy—which would include these vulnerable travellers—lies at the heart of the sin of Sodom.[8]

The Levite throws his concubine to the wolves (remember that Benjamin's sigil is the wolf! Here they come as a pack in the night) in his own stead, and she suffers the unimaginable all night long. The Benjamites make their statement. "When they get their hands on the traveller's concubine, and "know her" sexually, they will assert their "superiority" over the man, too. Controlling women is a mark of manhood in patriarchal societies,"[9] writes Frymer-Kensky.[10] When they are done, she crawls back to the doorstep and dies.[11] A Bethlehemite is abused and killed by Gibeahites, the Seed attacked by the Snake, just as David will be pursued by Saul.

An innocent child of Bethlehem is sacrificed, at night time, by an uncaring Levite, and in days to come Jesus, child of Bethlehem, will be sacrificed, at night time, by the Chief Priests, to suffer and to die in their place, to die so that they don't have to. Jesus of Bethlehem, who came into our world, received no hospitality, was treated shamefully, dominated and abused and left for dead—the ultimate victim of anti-hospitality at the cross. This woman, from the same village as Jesus, is a picture of Jesus.

When this story is set against the story of Ruth, which follows immediately after it, we see these contrasts in even starker relief. Bethlehem is honourably hospitable, Gibeah is shamefully inhospitable. Bethlehem is open to outsiders, Gibeah is aggressively xenophobic. Bethlehem treats women with respect. Both the Levite and the Gibeahites treat women as chattels, as non-persons. Treatment of women in Scripture is often indicative of how a society treats other disenfranchised or marginal groups, and in this, as in hospitality, Gibeah is found wanting. Yael Ziegler makes many of these observations:

> By comparing these two narratives, we observe that each of these stories is focused upon social interactions and contains several common motifs: food, the treatment of a vulnerable woman, and the ability (or inability) to recognize the Other as a subject, worthy

---

8. Kandiah, *God Is Stranger*, Kindle Location 919.

9. Frymer-Kensky, *Women of the Bible*, 124.

10. Frymer-Kensky is referring to toxic patriarchy, an abuse of power. Clearly, in the ideal social dynamic in many patriarchal cultures today, men use their power to protect, not to control, as in the case of Boaz with Ruth.

11. Thresholds had legal significance. The woman is indicting those within the house. Matthews, *Cultural World*, 149.

of a name and basic human rights. In fact, the social interactions may be viewed as the index of each of these narratives, representing the reason for the downfall of the Book of Judges and ultimately spurring the Book of Ruth toward effective leadership and a society in which recognition, continuity and stability can prevail.[12]

The other eleven tribes gather to punish the town of Gibeah, and tens of thousands die. The tribe of Benjamin is also invited to discipline this town within their borders, but they choose instead to protect their own against the "other." They won't extradite the Gibeahites to face justice. Thus, the nation is plunged into civil war, Benjamin against the other eleven. Judah leads the attack, both as the tribe who had been wronged, and also as God's nominated lead tribe. In Judges there are bookends about God's call on Judah to lead. In Judges 1:1–2 God says, "Judah shall arise." And in Judges 20:18, God repeats the command, "Judah shall arise." Yael Ziegler, commenting on 20:18, proposes that the chaos and difficulty throughout Judges all arises from Judah's failure to take a leading role.

> God's answer contains an implied rebuke: Had you only listened to Me in the beginning of the book, you would not have arrived at a situation in which you are fighting your own brethren, the Benjamites! God's answer and solution for the nation's future remains the same as before—the tribe of Judah must be appointed leader.[13]

The deeply tragic thing here is the scale of the revenge. Judah was originally appointed leader because of his *protection* of Benjamin. Here, he uses his authority to lead the armies in *destroying* Benjamin. Benjamin is a fierce, fighting tribe, and gives a good account of himself in the battle, but in the end, numbers tell against him. The body count is enormous. Only 600 men of an original 26,000 from the tribe of Benjamin are left alive.

> And the people of Israel had compassion for Benjamin their brother and said, "One tribe is cut off from Israel this day." Judges 21:6

When the adrenaline and blood have stopped flowing, in an act of reconciliation, the other tribes find a creative solution to build up the tribe of Benjamin again. The word in 21:6 translated "compassion" is *nacham*, which is the sound of breathing out, a deep sigh. It carries a spectrum of

12. Ziegler, *Ruth,* 57.
13. Ziegler, *Ruth,* 37.

emotional meanings, not least to rue or regret, or repent. It occurs again a few verses later, alongside *perez*, "to make a breach":

> And the people had compassion on Benjamin because the LORD
> had made a breach in the tribes of Israel. Judges 21:15

They had sworn an oath together that none of them would ever again give their daughters to marry Benjamites (21:1), so they provide a creative way around this vow, allowing for the Benjamites to take wives and begin to rebuild their tribe (21:7–12, 16–22). The shame, however, remains.

Gibeah in Benjamin will be remembered forever as a place of shame, of betrayal, a Sodom! When Saul, later, is chosen as king—a Benjamite from Gibeah—we readers are supposed to cry, "No! Not from there! Not a Benjamite! Not from Gibeah!"

Rachel's prophecy is coming true. Benjamin must bring suffering and division amongst the brothers. Jacob's prophecy is coming true. Judah must learn to lead, must be a lion. Once more, in this story, the tribe of Judah produces a sacrificial lamb, an innocent who dies at the hands of evil men. In sharp relief, the counter-cultural beauty of Bethlehem is revealed; in a world of distrust and brutality, a place of welcome and safety. In a world where the "other" is held at arm's length, Bethlehem opens her arms. In a world of shame, Bethlehem alone is honourable. In a world of objectification, Bethlehem alone dignifies. In a world of darkness, Bethlehem alone is light.

According to Salim Munayer, co-founder and director of the Musalaha ministry working on reconciliation between Israelis and Palestinians, ethical treatment of the "other" is a high priority in the Old Testament. In the Qur'an, too, we find suras demanding that foreigners be treated fairly and with respect. However, in both rabbinical Judaism and Islam, where the interpretive traditions carry much weight (*Talmud, Halacha, Hadith, Sharia*) the emphasis on hospitality, tolerance and equality is often ignored, and in some cases discrimination is encouraged.[14] The emphasis that is so prevalent in the Scripture is neglected in the tradition. This is a real danger. As the Christian church, we too have our own reprehensible back-catalogue of religiously endorsed anti-hospitality. The church has often tragically led the way in antisemitism, disgracefully discriminating against the Jewish minorities in Christian nations. The British church reacted poorly to the arrival of the "Windrush generation" from the Caribbean between

---

14. Munayer, "Theology of the Land," 259.

1948 and 1971, not welcoming newly arriving believers into the established Church. A large proportion of the South African church was associated with the discriminatory policies of *Apartheid*. We must ensure that the biblical emphasis on hospitality as an index of godliness is upheld, and that the shamefulness of anti-hospitality in all its manifestations is exposed.

8

Ruth

The House of Bread

> So Naomi returned, and Ruth the Moabite her daughter-in-law with her,
> who returned from the country of Moab. And they came to Bethlehem at
> the beginning of barley harvest.
>
> —RUTH 1:22

UP THE HILL TO Bethlehem trudge Ruth and Naomi. It's springtime in the House of Bread, just as the barley ripens for harvest, in late March or early April, golden and warm and joyful. Ruth is a refugee. She is a widow. And she is a Moabite. Her arrival, with Naomi, brings imbalance, a prickly feeling of discomfort, to the whole community. Studies of Ruth from the global South are sensitive to the communalistic dynamics of village life, and pick up on these themes. According to Jenkins, "In the global South, the book's interest lies in how the various characters faithfully fulfil their obligations to each other and their relatives. *What the North reads in moral or individualistic terms remains for the South social and communal.*"[1]

---

1. Jenkins, *New Faces*, 79–80. Italics mine.

The coolness of the welcome by the villagers is evident in 1:19b, "the whole town was stirred." Yael Ziegler sees this as a negative reaction by the townspeople. Her cultural insight into 1:19–21 is striking:

> We can deduce that there has been an antagonistic attitude on the part of the townswomen by observing Naomi's defensive response. . . . It is striking that no-one responds to Naomi's bitter, heart-breaking speech. The townspeople seem to gaze silently after her as Naomi trudges off in the aftermath of her painful monologue. In fact, the people of Bethlehem abandon Naomi to her fate. . . . No more words are exchanged between Naomi and her former neighbours until Boaz publicly marries Ruth, facilitating Naomi's newfound acceptance.[2]

The village women shun the new arrivals for several reasons. Naomi is treated coolly because she and Elimelech abandoned Bethlehem for Moab. Both women, as females dis-embedded from male protection (no father, husband, brother to vouch for them) could create trouble among the menfolk. And worst of all, Ruth is from Moab. In the text, she is repeatedly called "Ruth the Moabitess," as if to draw attention to her foreignness. This racist response is all the more heart-breaking because we are in Bethlehem! Vulnerable outsiders should receive a welcome here.

Moabite women were stereotyped as sexually promiscuous and therefore dangerous. The name of the people derives from *Me-Ab* ("from the father"), an appellation despising Moab's origins as incestuous. But when Lot's daughters slept with their father, they actually believed they were doing something heroic—they thought he was the only man left alive on the planet and they were preserving the human race (Gen 19:30–38)! When the men of Israel emerged from the wilderness, it was Moabite women who seduced them and led them into all manner of sins (Num 25:1–3). Hebrew mothers would gather up their sons and warn them against the women of Moab! And Ruth, an available young Moabite widow, is now loose in the village.

People who treat Ruth badly are written out of the story, a kind of narrative shunning. In chapter 2:5–6, the overseer makes a derogatory speech about Ruth, including un-called-for excessive references to her Moabite origin, and he is left unnamed and dropped from the story. Similarly, the other potential redeemer in chapter 4, who is called *Peloni Almoni*, or "Mr

2. Ziegler, *Ruth*, 169.

So-and-So," is left unnamed as a punitive strategy for his failure to take responsibility for Ruth. Ziegler, citing the Rabbi Rashi, notes:

> One who loses his name is one who does not deserve a name, either because he has sinned or because he did not fulfil his destiny, and instead shirked his responsibility. This would certainly seem to be the case with regard to the erstwhile redeemer, who shirks his responsibility. Rashi states this simply: "Peloni Almoni. His name was not written because he did not want to redeem" (Rashi 4:1).[3]

In a story where all the names have meanings, and where the word name *(shem)* is a leading word in chapter 4, appearing seven times, the narrator leaves people unnamed for their shameful, failed hospitality to Ruth. Once Boaz has taken responsibility for Ruth through marriage, the community dis-ease is resolved, a communal sigh of relief is breathed, and the women of the village can celebrate, re-opening communication with Naomi. It took the courageous, self-sacrificial action of this man of Judah, Boaz, to move towards the outsider and to remove this shame from the whole community. In a line of great venom-absorbers, Boaz absorbs the toxic shame surrounding Ruth, allowing, in the process, his own good name to be tarnished.

BOAZ' BRAVERY

The turning point in Ruth's story is 2:5. Until this point no-one has welcomed her into Bethlehem. In this verse, Boaz notices her, he sees her. His noticing of her transforms her from a non-person into someone with a future. "From the time that she entered Bethlehem, Ruth has not been acknowledged by the townspeople. . . . Boaz' query will begin to transform Ruth from a non-recognised stranger to a person with an identity."[4]

She has so many reasons to be invisible. Boaz, whose name means "strength," is portrayed as an honourable man. He is the son of Salmon, one of the leading families of Bethlehem, an owner of fields, an employer of labourers, and he has the influence to turn the elders away from their work during the busy harvest season in order to discuss the Ruth issue. In a world where reputation is currency, Boaz has much. He has much to lose.

3. Ziegler, *Ruth,* 374.
4. Ziegler, *Ruth,* 201.

In the Bible, privilege itself does not appear to be a bad thing. But privilege has the tendency to blind, to numb, to desensitise, to block the flow of hospitality, to "otherise." Boaz, however, is an example of someone who was able to marshal his resources to benefit the vulnerable. It must be stressed that these resources, primarily, were social capital—influence and a good name. Remember, honour was seen as the chief of virtues and the most desirable of prizes.

> A good name is to be chosen rather than great riches, and favour is better than silver or gold. Proverbs 22:1

Where the reader fails to see honour as primary, they will fail to see the reputational cost paid by Boaz in marrying a Moabite widow. Redemption always has a cost to the redeemer. Boaz paid dearly in the coin most precious in his context, and this what makes this ancestor of Christ a type, a prophetic pre-imaging, of Christ, whose death in shame absorbs and removes our shame, bringing us into his family (Heb 12:2).

This is most clear when we examine the contrast between Boaz and the erstwhile redeemer, "Mr So and So," in chapter 4. "Mr So and So," a nearer relative to Naomi, has the first option to purchase Elimelech's land, and he is prepared to do so until Boaz mentions Ruth.

> Then Boaz said, "The day you buy the field from the hand of Naomi, you also acquire Ruth the Moabite, the widow of the dead, in order to perpetuate the name of the dead in his inheritance." Ruth 4:5

"Ruth the Moabite widow? No way! You take the land. I am no longer interested!" declares the failed redeemer. Whatever precisely he refuses to accept here—marriage to a Moabitess, the production of mixed-race children, the dishonour of land being given through marriage to a foreigner, "Mr So and So's" refusal throws even more light on Boaz' counter-cultural acceptance. His selfishness is contrasted with Boaz' selfless action. Ziegler speaks of a "steep price" paid by Boaz: "Boaz is willing to pay a steep price, potentially sacrificing his reputation, and perhaps his economic situation."[5] Lau, the Hong Kongese theologian, concludes: "In the process of restoring or maintaining the lineage and name of Elimelech (4:10), he is simultaneously risking his own lineage and name. . . . Paradoxically, through his selfless actions his name is honoured and immortalised."[6]

5. Ziegler, *Ruth,* 407.
6. Lau, *Identity and Ethics,* 81.

Boaz is shamed in order that Ruth's shame might be removed. There is a costly, sacrificial nature to Boaz' action, the elevated one decreases in order that the lowly one might be increased. He loses by association with her, she gains by association with him. Yet, amidst the public perception of disgrace, there is a retrospective grant of honour, a collective sigh of relief at the resolution of a community problem, and ultimately a vindication by God, in the guise of offspring and royal lineage.

Boaz' venom absorption must not be underestimated. As with Mary's story later, the big problem in the story is shame, and the whole community is out of balance until the issue can be resolved. Boaz' bravery solves Ruth's problem, yes, but also brings resolution and peace to the whole village. And Boaz is a type of Jesus Christ.[7]

BOAZ' HOSPITALITY, OR GOD'S?

In the Megilloth, the five scrolls,[8] the absence of God is a significant theme.[9] There is little explicit mention of the action or intervention of God. The book of Ruth is no different—God seems to do very little directly. And yet God is working—through the agency of his people. This is communicated through ambiguity in the text. Are the wings of protection under which Ruth finds refuge Boaz' wings, as 3:9 suggests, or God's wings, as 2:12 claims? The answer is both—in Boaz' rescue and comfort of Ruth, God is rescuing and comforting Ruth. Again, it is unclear whether the *khesed* in 2:20 is Boaz' or God's. In the kindness of Boaz, God's kindness is on display. In the touch of Boaz, we see the touch of God. "The Ruth narrative shows that although God's direct actions can be sparse and mostly hidden, he works consistently and effectively *through* the godly actions of his people."[10]

The book of Ruth is therefore asking profound ethical questions. Mr So-and-So failed in his responsibility towards "the other" and lost his name. He is a warning. Boaz' bravery, however, is an example to be emulated.

7. For a fuller discussion of the dynamics of honour and shame in Ruth, see my MTh dissertation, McCullough, "Boaz' Bravery" (2019).

8. Ruth, Esther, Song of Songs, Ecclesiastes and Lamentations.

9. Eriksen & Davis, "Recent Research on the Megilloth," 307.

10. Lau and Goswell, *Unceasing Kindness,* 108.

REDEMPTION

Words related to redemption occur more than twenty times in the book of Ruth. "Redeemer" is a key biblical idea: those redeemed are often powerless or weak in some way—they need rescuing. And the most important thing about the redeemer is his kinship connection, he is a male relative who moves towards an imperiled family member and takes responsibility through costly action which removes shame and restores the family name. It is a transactional role, redeemers pay what cannot be paid. Thus, redeemers bought back family lands sold in times of hardship (Lev 25:23–38), paid the price for family members sold into slavery (Lev 25:47–49), avenged the blood of a murdered relative (Josh 20:2–9). Anything that threatened the family's good name, that brought imbalance, the redeemer acted to settle. He was a "relative who came to the rescue . . . the official guardian of the family's honour."[11]

The greatest Redeemer is God himself, who rescued Israel from Egypt. In Exodus 15:13–16, Moses praises the Lord's redemption of the people through his *khesed* and via a payment or purchase.[12] In the Psalms, God is frequently the redeemer both of individuals and of the nation.[13] In Isaiah and Jeremiah, the Lord promises to again redeem his people from the shame of exile and bring them home.[14]

These themes coalesce around Jesus Christ, whom the New Testament calls Redeemer (Rom 3:24, 8:23; 1 Cor 1:30; Eph 1:7, 4:30; Gal 4:4; Col 1:14; Titus 2:14; Heb 9:12). In Christ, descended from Boaz, born in Bethlehem, we Ruths find ourselves purchased, at great cost, by a relative, One who took flesh, who is not ashamed to call us brother (Heb 2:11–15), to rescue us from shame and give us a permanent place in his glorious family. It is Christ who takes responsibility for your honour.

HOUSE OF BREAD

Bethlehem as the House of Bread really comes to the fore in the Ruth story. The first chapter paints a stark contrast between Moab as a place of death and Bethlehem as a place of life and fruitfulness. After famine and hunger,

11. MacArthur, *Twelve Extraordinary Women*, 79.

12. For the kinship connection, see Exodus 4:22–23.

13. Lau and Goswell, *Unceasing Kindness*, 121.

14. E.g. Isaiah 62:12; Jeremiah 31:11.

Naomi and Ruth arrive in the village at the beginning of barley harvest. The story is replete with grain fields and harvest and early summer. Indeed, the whole story takes place over the seven weeks of the Counting of the Omer,[15] beginning at the barley harvest (Passover) and continuing until the wheat harvest (Pentecost).[16] Naomi and Ruth entered Bethlehem with heads bowed like the barley-ear, but by the wheat harvest their heads were erect with dignity like ears of wheat. In the Exodus, Passover is the moment of redemption and deliverance through the blood of lambs, Pentecost the occasion of the forging of a people at Sinai through the giving of Torah. For Ruth, her arrival at Bethlehem at Passover is her deliverance, and her marriage to Boaz at Pentecost her inclusion among the people of God. And for Ruth and Boaz' Seed, Jesus Christ, Passover is the occasion of deliverance for all Ruths at the crucifixion through the blood of the Lamb, and Pentecost the forging of one global people through the gift of the Holy Spirit.[17]

Boaz' sharing of bread and vinegar with Ruth (2:14) is taken by the Rabbis, not just as a sign of hospitality, but as a sign of kingship. Bread, a common Near Eastern metaphor for kingship, is understood this way in Ruth Rabba, as Ziegler explains:

> Bread is the mainstay of society, and a leader who can produce bread is an effective sustainer and protector. Bread is a symbol of effective leadership, and the one who offers bread is an effective leader. Boaz is the only human who gives bread in this story, and this momentous proffering of bread may well be interpreted as a hint that Boaz is extending the offer of kingship to Ruth.[18]

Indeed, Ruth forms a vital link between the time of the Judges, where there was no king, and 1 Samuel, where the king from Bethlehem will emerge. Ruth ends with a genealogy of David, making this connection explicit:

> Now these are the generations of Perez: Perez fathered Hezron,
> Hezron fathered Ram, Ram fathered Amminadab,
> Amminadab fathered Nahshon, Nahshon fathered Salmon,
> Salmon fathered Boaz, Boaz fathered Obed,
> Obed fathered Jesse, and Jesse fathered David. Ruth 4:18–22

15. See Deuteronomy 16:9–12 and Leviticus 23:15–22.

16. Both the Deuteronomy and the Leviticus stipulations include consideration for the sojourner and the widow as part of these harvests, as Boaz demonstrates.

17. Bull, *Love Song in Harvest*, 85–86.

18. Ziegler, *Ruth*, 228.

In this arrangement, starting with Tamar's son Perez, Boaz falls seventh and David falls tenth, both significant numbers. Schreiner, in his study tracking kingship through the Bible, puts the significance of Ruth like this:

> Surprisingly, Ruth forms a link in the chain that would bring David into the world, solving the problem of Judges, where Israel lacked a king. And a future son of David would bring many more Ruths, many more Gentiles into the fold of God's people, and fulfil the promise of universal blessing made to Abraham.[19]

TOWARDS KING DAVID

Aside from the genealogy, there are numerous resonances between the Ruth story and the story of David. Both Elimelech and David are specifically from the Ephrathite clan of Bethlehem (Ruth 1:2; 1 Sam 17:12). David sends his parents to Moab for safety, leaning on the kinship connection via his great-grandmother (1 Sam 22:3–4). Both stories have the wings of a garment as symbolic of patronage and protection at a pivotal moment (Ruth 2:12, 3:9; 1 Sam 15:27, 24:5). The exchange between David and the Philistine Ittai is redolent with the overtones of the scene between Ruth and Naomi (2 Sam 15:19–23; Ruth 1:8–18). Ruth, which starts with famine and ends with fulness, points towards the anointed king, David, who will bring fulness to his people, yet only temporarily. A later anointed king from Bethlehem will be the true bringer of rest.

In the little book of Ruth, we see Gentiles brought in, shame covered by the wings of God through his designated leader, sacrificial, lamb-like selflessness of a man of Bethlehem, love for enemies, the display of *khesed,* the House of Bread feeding the hungry, another courageous mother in Israel, the development of the story of the Seed, some hints towards kingship, and the powerful role of the Redeemer.

Boaz, whose mother Rahab was a recipient of divine hospitality, a receiver of unmerited grace, is now, as an insider to God's story, able to be a bestower, an agent of that same grace. This story is our story. We are Ruth, starved and seeking bread, vulnerable and seeking protection, adrift and seeking a home, ashamed and seeking shame-removal. And we are Boaz, recipients of grace now in a position to offer that same welcome to others,

---

19. Schreiner, *The King in his Beauty,* 135.

noticers of the invisible Ruths in our world, protectors of the vulnerable, champions of mercy, the hands and feet of God himself.

9

Saul
Wolf with a Spear

There was a man of Benjamin whose name was Kish, the son of Abiel, son of Zeror, son of Becorath, son of Aphiah, a Benjaminite, a man of wealth.

And he had a son whose name was Saul, a handsome young man. There was not a man among the people of Israel more handsome than he. From his shoulders upward he was taller than any of the people.

—1 SAMUEL 9:1–2

IN EVERY GENERATION, GOD's people have asked the leadership questions, "Who should bear authority? What is the nature of godly influence? Who is, and, conversely, who is not qualified for such a role?" One of the Bible's most ancient yet straightforward ways to answer this question is by means of *contrast*. Two characters are presented, often antagonistic, with Scripture honouring the one and humiliating the other. And in almost every case, the small is chosen over the mighty, the naturally-despised over the humanly-qualified. From virtually the first pages of the Bible, this dialectic is on show. The display of this truth is fundamental to the Bethlehem story.

Power-sensitivity is not a new thing, not unique to our "woke" post-modern twenty-first century, not new in our post-colonial world order. That God resists the proud and gives grace to the humble is wisdom as ancient as the world.

First, we are shown Cain and Abel. Cain, meaning "Producer," worked the land like his father. Abel, meaning "meaningless," or "breath" (the same word as in Ecclesiastes—"everything is meaningless"), was a despised shepherd. When God accepted Abel's offering and not Cain's, "Cain was confronted with God's measure of what truly matters and what is truly great,"[1] he felt anger and shame, and he murdered his brother. This story is about brotherliness; the word "brother" occurs seven times in Genesis 4:1–11. In all these verses, Cain is never called Abel's brother. Cain *has* a brother but *is not* a brother. "Am I my brother's keeper?" (a pun on shepherd—Abel was a keeper of sheep) is a rhetorical question to which the answer is supposed to be "yes!" This story re-values what is important. Life is not assessed on production but on brotherliness. In the New Testament, Cain is remembered as an example of failed leadership (1 John 3:12; Jude 1:11), whilst Abel is praised as one who still speaks—an influence that outlives him (Heb 11:4).

A similar contrast is painted between Nimrod and Abram (Genesis 10–12). Nimrod is a mighty man, Abram from a genetic cul-de-sac; Nimrod a founder of cities, Abram a leaver of cities; Nimrod's narrative dominated by "come"—a gatherer, Abram's narrative dominated by "go"—as one obediently scattered by God. Nimrod's project meets divine displeasure, and God turns away from the city, finds a small man on the margins, and designates him Seed-bearer.[2]

Again, the twins Jacob and Esau will spend their lives in competition and rivalry. The contrast in their physique and personalities is absolute. Esau is full of testosterone, an Alpha male, a hunter (like Nimrod, an epithet worthy of great honour in many societies), beloved of his father. Jacob, in every possible way, is the compete opposite. Yet thanks to the sovereign grace of God in election, primogeniture is once again over-turned and the Seed-promise passes to the younger son.

This narrative technique of presenting two examples, one honourable, one shameful, one humanly qualified, the other divinely ordained, is most fully rounded-out in the tension between Saul and David.

1. Volf, *Exclusion and Embrace*, 95.
2. McCullough, *Global Humility*, 83–92.

When Saul is presented to the people in 1 Samuel 9:1–2, they accept him for three reasons. His family is wealthy. He is handsomer than anyone in Israel. And he is gigantically tall. This combination of material and physical resources rendered him untouchable in the kingship stakes—the equivalent of the British romantic ideal, "tall, dark and handsome." According to the standards of the age, a natural-born leader.

For all this, there is a glaring warning in verse 1, where is it twice mentioned that Saul is a Benjamite. Not just a Benjamite, we will discover, but from Gibeah. "No!" the people are supposed to cry, hackles raised, warning bells clanging, remembering their history. "Not a Wolf! Not a Benjamite! Not from Gibeah!" But they forget the warnings of history. Overwhelmed by their desire for a king, blinded by Saul's charisma and vigour, they clamour for his coronation. Every generation makes this mistake. The selection of leaders according to the cultural ideals of the age, rather than the initiative of God's Spirit, has always been a problem for God's people.

The story of Saul is the story of leadership according to the flesh; of human ability and prowess, and it is a tragic story. It is the opposite of the narrative of Messiah, the narrative of weakness and disdain, the atmosphere of Bethlehem. And as flesh wars against Spirit, so Saul wars against David, Benjamin against Judah, Gibeah against Bethlehem.

Saul starts out by losing his donkeys. Donkeys are a picture of kingship. Judah, in his kingship prophecy, was promised donkeys (Genesis 49:11).[3] If Saul can't even look after a few donkeys, how will he lead a nation?

A WOLF WITH A SPEAR

Often when we meet Saul, he has a spear in his hand. "Characters," writes Leithart, "were marked as good or bad by the weapons they used and how they used them."[4] Jewish scholar Robert Alter suggests that Bible characters often seem to be associated with an object that serves as a metaphor for their life. Jacob keeps using stones,[5] and he is the foundation-stone of the nation. Samson is associated with fire,[6] which suits his personality as an unpredictable, uncontrollable force. And Saul uses weapons, in particular

---

3. See also 1 Kings 1:33–44; Zechariah 9:9.

4. Leithart, *Son to Me*, 89.

5. Alter, *The Five Books of Moses*, 100.

6. Alter, *Prophets*, 130.

his beloved spear. If he had a family coat of arms, it would be a wolf with a spear.[7]

Saul, like so many leaders after him, thinks that leadership is through force, coercion, might. David stands in direct opposition to this. When David volunteers to fight Goliath, Saul covers him in armour. Goliath has so much weaponry that it takes several verses to describe it all, and Saul feels that force must be met with force. David not only rejects Saul's offer of arms, he goes out to fight Goliath dressed as a shepherd.

> Then he took his staff in his hand and chose five smooth stones from the brook and put them in his shepherd's pouch. His sling was in his hand, and he approached the Philistine. 1 Samuel 17:40

His staff, like his ancestor Judah's staff, like the staff of Moses, is a shepherd's emblem of authority. Seale observes that the staff is ubiquitous to nomadic shepherds in the region today.

> The nomad's inseparable companion is his stick or staff. It was literally a basic piece of equipment which he put to a hundred daily uses . . . He leans on it to rest himself; he beats down leaves for fodder; he throws it across his shoulder and hangs from it his tools and utensils; he plants it in the sand, throws his cloak over it, and thus provides himself with a patch of shade; when lighting a fire, he lays it on the ground and uses the end where it bifurcates as a support for his flints; it extends his bucket rope for him to reach down a well to deep water. Finally, in an emergency, it served as a weapon.[8]

The stones are placed in his explicitly described "shepherd's pouch." David raises his voice loud enough for Goliath to hear, loud enough for Saul to hear, loud enough for the listening ranks of Israel to hear and understand, and like a prophet denounces reliance on weaponry.

> Then David said to the Philistine, "You come to me with a sword and with a spear and with a javelin, but I come to you in the name of the LORD of hosts, the God of the armies of Israel, whom you have defied . . . and that all this assembly may know that the LORD saves not with sword and spear. For the battle is the LORD's, and he will give you into our hand." 1 Samuel 17:45, 47

---

7. Leithart, *House*, 33.

8. Seale, *Desert Bible*, 80.

David is not just speaking to the Philistine giant, he is speaking to the Israelite giant too. Swords and spears are no match for the anointed shepherd who comes in the name of the Lord. He's rebuking Saul the spear-lover in the hearing of all Israel.

One night, on one of the many occasions when Saul and his army head out into the desert to pursue David, we are shown a classic tableau of Saul, asleep in the centre of the camp, with his spear stuck in the ground at his head, and the army encamped around him (1 Sam 26:7). On their previous wilderness journeys, God's people had been taught clearly that *God* is supposed to be in the centre of the encampment. The sense is clear: Saul thinks that he and his spear are God. David and Abishai steal into the camp, tiptoeing past the sleeping sentries, and steal Saul's spear. In one stroke, David demonstrates that Saul's armies and weapons are powerless, and symbolically takes the kingdom away from Saul.

ENVY: SAUL PUTS HIS EYE ON DAVID

First Samuel 18:6–15 shows the increasing anger, paranoia and violence which arose in Saul when he "eyed David from that day on." As soon as David's rising popularity was articulated as measurable, score-able honour ("tens of thousands" versus Saul's "thousands"), Saul fixed his eye on David, a certain reference to envy. Eyes and envy are deeply connected in Middle Eastern thought,[9] and throughout Scripture. Saul's torment is exacerbated by an evil spirit. Envy is one of the few sins explicitly connected with demonic influence in Scripture. Isaiah 14:12–15, in which Christian tradition sees the story of the devil, is replete with competitive, dissatisfied, covetous envy. The Snake envies the Seed. Rejected one envies Anointed One. Saul throws his spear at David. Herod throws his kill-team at Jesus. And, according to both Matthew and Mark, it was out of envy that the chief priests delivered Jesus up to Pilate to be put to death. Anointing attracts the eye of the devil. Competition is the great enemy of grace. For Saul, now, there was no going back on his obsession with killing David.

When Saul is finally declared rejected, we are not surprised. In 1 Samuel 15, we are twice told that the Lord "regretted" or "was grieved over" Saul's kingship. *Nacham* is a word like a sigh of regret, a saddened expulsion of breath. The last time God was *nacham* was in the days of Noah, leading to the flood and a new beginning through Noah the Seed—de-creation

9. Malina, *New Testament World*, 120.

and recreation. In the same way, Saul's kingdom will at this point enter the trauma of civil war, flailing about in its death throes, until the re-creation to be brought about by David, descendant of Noah, of the Seed-family, of Bethlehem.

In the end, Saul dies by his own steel. He falls on his own sword, and then the Philistines cut off his head. Jesus will later teach his own disciples that "those who draw the sword shall die by the sword"—Saul is a case in point. The Philistines behead him as revenge for the decapitation of Goliath, an Israelite giant head for a Philistine one. His beloved armour is put on display in the temple of Ashtaroth (1 Sam 31:10)—proof that sword and spear and breastplate cannot protect God's people. The sheep of Israel are scattered. The land waits.

Leithart wonderfully captures the poetry of this contrast between David and Saul:

> Saul and David were contrasted by what they held in their hand: Saul held the spear, while David held the harp. The hand that holds the spear cannot grasp the harp player. And eventually, the one holding the spear would be left empty-handed, while the one with the harp would grasp a kingdom.[10]

In a provocative anecdotal postscript, the author of 2 Samuel takes one last shot at Saul's spear-reliance.

> And he struck down an Egyptian, a handsome man. The Egyptian had a spear in his hand, but Benaiah went down to him with a staff and snatched the spear out of the Egyptian's hand and killed him with his own spear. 2 Samuel 23:21

The handsome Egyptian with spear in hand is like handsome Saul—Saul is compared to an Egyptian, the oppressors of God's people. Benaiah, conversely, had a staff, the shepherd's *shevet* of messianic kingship, promised to Judah in Genesis 49:10 and prophesied by Balaam in Numbers 24:17, the staff used by God himself as he shepherds his people in Psalm 23:4 and 45:6. Staff beats spear, shepherd trumps warrior, and the Egyptian has his own spear turned against him. The Shepherd's staff goes on to be an explicitly messianic emblem, in Psalm 2:9, Isaiah 11:4 and Micah 7:14. God's anointing is with the shepherd from Bethlehem, his staff becoming a sceptre. And those who wield the spear will die by it.

---

10. Leithart, *Son to Me,* 131.

10

David
Rise of the Shepherd

Now, therefore, thus you shall say to my servant David, "Thus says the LORD of hosts, I took you from the pasture, from following the sheep, that you should be prince over my people Israel."

—2 SAMUEL 7:8

UP THE HILL TO Bethlehem climbed the long-haired, aging prophet Samuel, a horn full of olive oil slung round his neck, leading a heifer behind him. His cover story was a sacrifice, inviting all the village elders. His real purpose, the voice of God echoing in his ears and in his spirit, was to find one of these elders, Jesse son of Obed, grandson of Boaz, and to anoint one of his sons king. This is treason, hence the trembling of the village elders— why is the great prophet and judge of Israel coming to interfere with our affairs? We are just a quiet community minding our own business. Keep your politics out of our village!

The entire narrative of 1 Samuel 16:1–13 is one of the unlikely choosing of God. Bethlehem, quiet village that didn't want any trouble. Jesse, with Canaanite and Moabite blood in his veins, not the purest of Jewish

DNA. Rudeness, making all the village elders wait while someone runs out into the fields to find David. Irony, the mention of Jesse's seven sons passing before Samuel, and none of them being the chosen one. Seven is the number of completeness. Jesse has a perfect batch of sons. Eighth is superfluous, overlooked, uninvited. The shepherding role given to the youngest, the despised, the uneducated, as shepherds have always been regarded. When we first meet David he is in the field faithfully keeping his father's sheep, as later Bethlehem shepherds will be when angelic choirs sing. God rebukes Samuel for being obsessed with tallness, a reference to his mistake in choosing Saul,

> But the LORD said to Samuel, "Do not look on his appearance or on the height of his stature, because I have rejected him. For the LORD sees not as man sees: man looks on the outward appearance, but the LORD looks on the heart." 1 Samuel 16:7

And David, the Eighth-born, the Overlooked, the Uninvited is anointed before his brothers and the village elders. He is chosen from the margins of the world, and the Holy Spirit comes upon him. He is the anointed one—Messiah.

This scene is counter-cultural to almost any place. David, the wrong geography, the wrong family, the wrong age, and yet God chooses him. For readers in the Middle East, for the youngest son to be promoted above his brothers is almost unthinkable. And yet, in the wider scheme of things, we are expecting a leader from Judah, we have been introduced to this family through Rahab and Ruth, and we are well within the great narrative arc of the Bible. This is David's vertical introduction, his choosing by God.

SEED VERSUS SNAKE

Next, we witness David's horizontal introduction, when he is noticed by all Israel. David's first words in all of Scripture are filled with the language of shame-removal.

> And David said to the men who stood by him, "What shall be done for the man who kills this Philistine and takes away the reproach from Israel? For who is this uncircumcised Philistine, that he should defy the armies of the living God?" 1 Samuel 17:26

Reproach (*cherpah*) and defy (*charap*) both come from the same root, a shame of uncleanness and disempowerment. Israel, occupied by the unclean, uncircumcised Philistines, is humiliated, and needs ridding of this blight, this stain.

One of the things that heroes do is to remove shame. National saviours have frequently used ethnic humiliation at the hands of a foreign power as a rallying cry. The Chinese revolution, for example, leveraged the national sense of shame to fuel anti-Western sentiment. At the entrance to the parklands of the Summer Palace, there is still a sign saying, "Do not forget the national shame, rebuild the Chinese nation."[1] Shepherds remove shame from their people, as Boaz does for Ruth, as Joseph does for Mary, as David will do for Mephibosheth. Bethlehem is a locus of shame-removal, and mission done the Bethlehem way will seek to deliver people from the shame of disempowerment, dispossession and dislocation. Ultimately, Jesus comes to deliver his people from the spectre of inevitability casting its long shadow of hopelessness, and to give them a liberty which means they can hold their heads high. Shepherds remove shame.

We saw in the last chapter that David fights Goliath dressed as a shepherd, and using shepherds' weapons, eschewing Saul's reliance on iron and bronze. Goliath is a giant, who wears scaly armour like a snake (1 Sam 17:5), a manifestation of *the* Snake.[2] Here we have the Seed versus the Snake. Goliath is descended from the Anakim whom Joshua defeated. The 40-day face-off in the wilderness is like the 40 years the people spent in the desert. Every generation has its own giants to fight, and David is a new Joshua. King Saul is supposed to fight Goliath, giant to giant, champion to champion. Where he fails, David steps in. Once again, Judah is a substitute for failed Benjamin. Judah will begin leading here as he is destined to do.

David turns up at the battle, faithfully obeying his father, looking after his sheep. He brings as a gift for the commander ten loaves and ten cheeses, tokens of Bethlehem. The loaves (*lechem*) are from the House of Bread and the sheep's milk cheeses are from the House of Meat (1 Sam 17:17–18). The narrator fills this story with shepherding and Bethlehem language. David stones Goliath to death for blasphemy. The giant falls facedown and his head is cut off—exactly as the statue of Dagon, whom Goliath worshipped, had fallen before the ark of the Lord (1 Sam 5). David here, full of the Spirit of the Lord, is like the ark, a carrier of the Presence, and Goliath must fall before him. Saul also, when he dies, will be decapitated and have his armour stripped from him. David, in time, will see both Philistine giant

1. Mishra, *Ruins of Empire*, 288.
2. Roberts & Wilson, *Echoes of Exodus*, Kindle Location 1050.

and Israelite giant fall, and he will be the last man standing. The Snake is defeated by the Seed through a head-wound, fulfilling, albeit partially, Genesis 3:15.[3]

WILDERNESS

It is not possible to understand David without realising that the wilderness was a big part of his life. As a Bethlehem shepherd, he would have followed the customary semi-nomadic rhythms, spending the winter months out in the wilderness grazing the flocks far and wide, returning to Bethlehem in March or April for lambing and then remaining close to Bethlehem's water supply through the long, dry months until October.[4] He knew the Judean wilderness intimately, which is how he was able to retreat into its fastnesses during his outlaw years, using it as a buffer against Saul. The vast rocky desert harbours him, welcomes him into its bosom, keeps him safe from Saul. In the wilderness, David always seems at home, at his best, with home court advantage, while Saul seems out of his depth, exposed. This ability to "go Bedouin" temporarily has political advantages, even in the Middle East in recent times. J.T. Luke writes,

> Occasionally village folk took to Bedouin life to evade conscription, or to flee from tribute, taxes, blackmail, debts or drought. Sometimes, too, criminals might turn Bedouin, having perforce left their villages after committing murder or other crimes. Tribal tradition frequently has it that a certain tribe or family is of non-nomadic origin and at a certain time has gone over to the Bedouin way of life.[5]

Rabbi Danya Ruttenberg writes of the importance of wilderness—*midbar*—in the Jewish tradition:

> It's no coincidence that everything important in the Bible—prophecies, kingships, Torah—came out in the wilderness. It's a place of danger and vulnerability, and perhaps feels like it can go on

---

3. Leithart observes the frequency of "death by head wound in the Old Testament. Sisera, Abimelech, Goliath, Absalom – many of the enemies of God have their heads crushed. When a scene or event is repeated in this way, it is deliberate and theologically grounded. All these are types of the serpent, whose head the Seed of the woman will crush." Leithart, *House*, 34.

4. Gottwald, *Tribes*, 449.

5. Luke, *Pastoralism and Politics*, 84–85.

forever. . . . And in that liminality, in the quiet—we make ourselves ready to hear the voice of God.[6]

That's where David learned to hear God. In the Judean wilderness. As long as David is desert-based, he seems to be "a man after God's own heart." Once he takes Jerusalem and tries to be a city-king, his story unravels. There is a profound lesson here for the people of God: the exposure and unpredictability of the wilderness is our home, for it is there that we learn to depend on God. The gods of order and system and control are not our gods. Indeed, as Elie Khoury proposes, the transition from a wilderness-life led by the shepherd-God Yahweh to a settled life in Canaan proved problematic for the Hebrews. Yahweh was (wrongly) conceived as being the God of rocks and desert only, whereas Baal, the god of Canaan, was all about the order of a settled annual harvest cycle.[7] This is where syncretism begins, in the transition from desert to sown.[8]

Of course, the Lord had purposed a settled inheritance for his people, and their finding a home in Canaan was God's idea. And yet, much seems to have been built into their new, settled lives in order to keep the desert traditions alive; the Feast of Tabernacles, the credal statement of origins, "A wandering Aramean was my father" (Deut 26:5). It is as if God was giving his people liturgical reminders to safeguard them against the arrogance and presumption that settled prosperity would surely bring.

It was in this wilderness context that David wrote the celebrated Psalm 23, "The Lord is my shepherd." His ancestor Jacob was the first to observe this divine shepherding, in Genesis 48:15, and the shepherd-metaphor for God developed during Israel's wilderness years, as they were led through the desert for 40 years. The Bethlehem shepherd motif remains consistent through Micah 5, Ezekiel 34, and through to the birth of the Good Shepherd, descended from David, announced to shepherds in those same fields.

The desert toughened David. Thompson, acquainted with the region a century ago, observed that same hardiness in Bethlehemites in his day:

It is asserted in this country that there is something in the water of certain places which renders the people sturdy, hard, and fearless;

6. Rabbi Danya Ruttenberg's Twitter feed, April 30th, 2019. https://twitter.com/TheRaDR/status/1123283622973325312

7. Kedourie, *The Jewish World*, 46.

8. Both David and Saul demonstrate this syncretism in the naming of their sons: both have one son based on the divine name and one based on Baal, Saul's being Eshbaal and Jonathan, David's being Beliada and Jedediah.

and it is curious enough that people of this character have ever been connected with Bethlehem. David and his family, his mightiest captains, Joab and others, came from it, and they were fierce, terrible men. . . Seated on the summit-level of the hill-country of Judah, with deep gorges descending east to the Dead Sea, and west to the plains of Philistia, the shepherds of Bethlehem had to contend not only with bears and lions, whose dens were in those wild wadies, but also with human enemies—the Philistines on the west, and Arab robbers on the east. They would, therefore, from childhood, be accustomed to bear fatigue, hunger, heat and cold, both by night and by day, and also to brave every kind of danger, and fight with every kind of antagonist.[9]

ADULLAM

In his flight from Saul, David goes down to the caves at Adullam (1 Sam 22:1). This extensive cave-system, now a national park, is an ideal guerrilla base, just where the hills begin to rise into the Judean Highlands. Adullam is five miles from where David slew Goliath, and twelve miles from Bethlehem. On a visit today one can explore numerous caves and subterranean tunnels that have been carved out of the limestone over the ages in order to give shelter to rebels. Many of these can be traced to the Bar Kokhba revolt, when Jewish freedom-fighters were hiding from the Romans in AD 132–135. With Adullam as his base, David begins to gather his Judahite core, "everyone who was in distress, and everyone who was in debt, and everyone who was bitter in soul" (1 Sam 22:2). A lot of Judah's menfolk were struggling under the reign of Saul, who favoured his own tribe. David begins learning how to shepherd the downtrodden sheep of Judah, other men from the underside of the world—how similar to the beginning of the ministry of his illustrious descendant Jesus, who "had compassion on them, because they were like sheep without a shepherd" (Mark 6:34)!

Caves in the Bible often represent death, as they were used as tombs.[10] This is the lowest point on David's story-arc, his burial in Adullam, the Seed being planted in the wilderness. This scene is graphically contrasted within a few verses with Saul, under a tree (not in the wilderness), with his spear in his hand, surrounded by the men of Benjamin, dishing out lands and

---

9. Thompson, *The Land and the Book,* 2:509.

10. Leithart, *Son to Me,* 128.

honours (22:6–7). There is a clear Exodus-theme for David as he embodies Israel's story. He is a shepherd oppressed and pursued by an evil king (as the Hebrews, who were shepherds in Egypt, were pursued by Pharaoh). There is a Passover-type moment at the end of 1 Samuel, when Saul eats a meal of unleavened bread and meat in the middle of the night at the house of the witch in Endor. The following day, Saul dies—like the death of the firstborn of the Egyptians—and after this David begins his ascent to his kingdom. David experiences flight into the wilderness, miraculous provision of bread, and an eventual triumphal entry into the promised land.

> Saul is the new Pharaoh. Like Pharaoh, Saul tries to kill the anointed leader while he is still young, but fails, ironically through the intervention of his own daughter. Like Pharaoh, Saul brings his adversary into his household. Like Pharaoh, Saul's attempts to destroy his rival lead to an escape at night-time, through the substitution of an animal (1 Sam. 19:11–17). Like Pharaoh, Saul hardens his heart and pursues his opponent, to the eventual destruction of both himself and his family. David, meanwhile, flees the pursuing king and ends up wandering in the wilderness.[11]

Looking forward to Christ, David goes through a death-and-resurrection experience from Adullam, through the wilderness, and finally to his throne. Just as Judah learned that leadership is through suffering, so does David. We recall Leithart's comments from Genesis 35:

> Judah was proclaimed the royal tribe only after he had offered himself as a substitute for Benjamin. Similarly, Saul became king without ever accepting the cross, while David, the king from Judah, rose to the throne only after a death and resurrection.[12]

JESUS, SON OF DAVID

There are potentially infinite ways in which David is a type, or forerunner, of his descendant Jesus Christ. Both are born in Bethlehem, and both die in Jerusalem. Both were shepherd-kings. Both have a long-haired Nazirite prophet preparing their way: barren Hannah births Samuel who anoints David, and barren Elizabeth births John the Baptist who is present at Jesus' anointing. In fact, Samuel and John are the only two Hebrew prophets

11. Roberts & Wilson, *Echoes of Exodus,* Kindle Location 1060.

12. Leithart, *Son to Me,* 76.

whose birth and death are both narrated in Scripture.[13] Both David and Jesus are Messiahs (anointed ones), full of the Holy Spirit, with authority over evil spirits. Both had significant involvement with Gentiles—as much as David is celebrated by modern Zionists as the model of Israelite purity, he had mixed ancestry, mixed marriages, mixed political alliances, and many non-Jews even within his personal guard. Both had the wilderness in their souls. David battled a snake-giant and an Israelite giant who envied him and sought to kill him. Jesus battled the Snake, as well as the Jerusalem authorities who envied him and sought to kill him. In both stories, those who draw the sword will die by the sword.

Both David and Jesus had as their great motivation the removal of the power of shame, and the creation of a free people who can hold their heads high with dignity. In the David story, there is a false king ruling the land (Saul) and the snake goes unconfronted. David from Bethlehem is selected and anointed. There is a period of envy-fuelled persecution, resulting in a burial of the Seed in Adullam, around which broken people gather, and finally a subsequent resurrection and enthronement. In the Jesus story, the false king is Herod, the envy-fuelled persecution is by the Jerusalem elite (early on Herod and later the chief priests), broken people gather around his death and burial, the planting of the Seed, and celebrate his subsequent resurrection, ascension and enthronement.

Jesus, in so many ways, is the son of David. The great difference is that the David kingdom unravels again, while the Jesus kingdom will endure forever. This difference is hugely significant, and the unravelling of the David story is a highly instructive part of the whole. Not until Jesus will all of the Bethlehem themes come together in one glorious fulfilment. Until then, every generation will face its giants, suffer under imperfect leaders, and struggle to be truly free from shame.

13. Caiger, *Lives of the Prophets*, 27.

11

David
Oh, How I Long . . .

David was then in the stronghold, and the garrison of the Philistines was
then at Bethlehem.

And David said longingly, "Oh, that someone would give me water to
drink from the well of Bethlehem that is by the gate!"

Then the three mighty men broke through the camp of the Philistines
and drew water out of the well of Bethlehem that was by the gate and
carried and brought it to David. But he would not drink of it. He poured it
out to the LORD

and said, "Far be it from me, O LORD, that I should do this. Shall I drink
the blood of the men who went at the risk of their lives?"

—2 SAMUEL 23:14–17

IN THE MIDDLE EAST, warfare is all about strategic control of water resources. Any commander knows that access to water is literally a matter of life or
death. In Palestine, rivers can run in the valleys during the rainy season but
dry up during the summer. Five long months of no precipitation, beginning

in May at harvest time and continuing, parched and sweltering, until October. Bethlehem had the natural strategic advantage of being on a hilltop, hence defensible, as well as having its own springs. That's part of the reason for its longevity. So in this story, it is natural that the Philistines should take Bethlehem and then garrison there; well-watered high ground from which to foray into the surrounding areas.

Part of Bethlehem's strategic importance has always been its water supply. Archaeologist Nigro identifies six springs which have watered the village for millennia; "Water supply in Bethlehem is assured by several sources distributed in its immediate surroundings. Six main springs are known: 'Ain Umm al-Daraj; 'Ain Artas; 'Ain Salih; 'Ain Faruja; 'Ain Attan; 'Ain Battir, which gave a valid supply to the communities living in the area since the 4th millennium BC onwards."[1]

Herod the Great, taking advantage of Roman technology and cheap labour, would later construct long aqueducts from Bethlehem to both Jerusalem and Herodion, his obscenely expensive man-made mountain-fortress vanity-project. Jerusalem needed expanding because the religious tourism revenues would be a significant budget line for Herod's coffers, but Jerusalem is limited to only one natural spring, Siloa, which could not possibly support the expansion which Herod was proposing. The functioning of Herod's temple would demand massive amounts of water to wash away all the blood from the sacrifices, as well as sustaining the growing population of the city. Much of this water came from Bethlehem. The growth of the centre always commandeers resources from the margins. Bethlehem paid; empire profited. This the direct opposite of the kingship ideal, where king feeds people. Here people are feeding king.

Bethlehem has resisted this co-option of its water supply on and off over the centuries. In AD 70, Jewish zealots destroyed the aqueduct in a guerrilla attack on the Roman presence, forcing Rome to re-build it.[2] After the drought of 1900–01, the Jerusalem officials sought to rebuild the "lower aqueduct," which since the time of Herod has brought water through a series of tunnels from Bethlehem to Jerusalem. Masterman reports that, "when repaired it was wilfully damaged by the Fellahin of Bethlehem, who strongly object to the diversion to Jerusalem of what they have come to consider their special water supply."[3]

1. Nigro, "Bronze and Iron Ages," 3.
2. Raheb & Strickert, *Bethlehem 2000*, 69.
3. Masterman, "Water Supply of Jerusalem," 110.

Throughout the subsequent history of Palestine, whoever would conquer Jerusalem must first take Bethlehem, cutting off the water supply so that the city could not hold out under siege. Most recently, the British army did exactly that, cutting off the water supply from Bethlehem on December 7th, 1917, and taking Jerusalem four days later.

The State of Israel's renewed modern interest in Bethlehem is for exactly the same reasons—for strategic control of water. Bethlehem-born Christian priest Mitri Raheb writes:

> The control of water under Israeli occupation is a continuation of this imperial natural resource strategy. Israel uses over 80 per cent of the natural water resources of the West Bank, leaving only 20 percent to the native Palestinians. The locations of Israeli settlements in the West Bank are established upon the land's natural aquifers. A close look at where the wall is being built shows that its location has less to do with "security concerns" and more with a massive land-and-water grab. . . . Significantly, the amount of water available to an Israeli settler in the West Bank is four times that available to a Palestinian.[4]

In our passage of Scripture, which took place in the days when David was still a rebel leader based out of Adullam, this is exactly the situation being faced. It's harvest time (May), with the long dry summer stretching ahead. Adullam, which was probably an ideal guerrilla base in the winter months, would provide no water during the summer. Strategically, militarily, David and his men need to secure access to water if they are going to survive the summer.

For David, the strategic imperative is compounded by an emotional burden. His home village is occupied by the Philistine soldiers. With all the menfolk off fighting (most of those joining the rebellion were his kin), David's female relatives, aunts and cousins and fellow villagers, would be at the mercy of these soldiers.

And the emotional burden is compounded by shame. The shame of powerlessness, of having one's ancestral village overrun by uncircumcised Philistines, the pollution and affront to his honour that David would have felt. If shame is a form of imbalance, David needs to act to correct the balance, to gain satisfaction, to rescue his village.

The impression arising from David's cry, "Oh, that someone would give me water to drink from the well of Bethlehem that is by the gate!" is

---

4. Raheb, *Empire*, 58.

one of a ferment all of these emotions. Lying parched in the heat, severely dehydrated, through cracked and blistered lips we hear him expressing his pent-up frustration and concern and shame. He remembers the sweet waters of his childhood. Perhaps he is already in a delirium, muttering under his breath, as nostalgic visions of a simpler time, a time of innocence, dance before his eyes.

This cry resonates through the ages with all the dispossessed. For the millions on our planet who have been forcibly de-coupled from their motherland, who can never again drink the water from the wells their grandparents dug, whose houses are lived in by strangers and whose trees are harvested by outsiders, David's pain is their pain. His nostalgia, their nostalgia. His thirst, their thirst.

David's three mighty men, none of whom, as far as we know, were Bethlehemites themselves, confer amongst themselves. They come up with a daring plan. Relying on the element of surprise, they will fight uphill to Bethlehem, through the Philistine lines, draw water—a slow process and fraught with danger from a manually-operated well—and carry it back to their chief. This is a last-gasp grab for water, a do-or-die mission. Such initiative, risk and courage does not result from their fear of David as chief. They are not just servicing a whim of his fancy. They love him. They will risk their lives to keep him alive. If this is a lesson in leadership and loyalty, then it teaches us that David's men genuinely loved him. Leaders that engender sacrificial love and loyalty are rare—in any generation and in any culture.

Their "breaking through" of the Philistine lines is described with a big Bible word—*baqa*. *Baqa* is the word for the splitting of the Red Sea. It is the word for God's cleaving of the rock in the wilderness to bring forth water. *Baqa* is the piercing of an obstacle in order to achieve deliverance.

The mighty men pierce enemy lines, secure a skin of precious water, and carry it back to David at the rebel hideout. Careful of each drop that may spill, they carry the water twelve miles back to Adullam and offer it to David.

He stirs, and opens his eyes. He is touched by their loyalty, by their sacrifice. His swollen tongue sticks to the roof of his mouth, and the smell of the water is like a physical blow to his senses. Summoning his last vestiges of vital force David sits up, takes the water vessel from the hands of his loyal captains and . . .

David pours the water on the ground. He pours it out to the Lord. It is an offering to God, a libation. To worship is to hand something precious over to God. David was a worshipper.

As the water snakes away along the rocks on the valley floor, and the mighty men look on in disbelief, David explains his reasoning. "Far be it from me, O LORD, that I should do this. Shall I drink the blood of the men who went at the risk of their lives?" He refuses to be the kind of general who benefits from other people's risk, calling this "drinking their blood." To drink someone's blood is to gain life from their sacrifice. To get stronger while they get weaker. That's what Christians will do a thousand years later—drink the blood of David's great son. Gain life from his death. Get strong because he got weak.

David's cry, "Oh, that someone would give me water to drink from the well of Bethlehem!" prophetically voices the cry of all mankind. Mankind, lying parched and dying, thirsty for the water of life, cries in anguish for the only water that can truly satisfy, the water of life, whose source is Bethlehem. Jesus of Bethlehem, the only one who can quench our deepest needs. Some older Christian commentators saw in this story a prophecy of Christ, as Leithart has captured:

> If we take the story this way, David's decision to pour out the water may also have typological associations. Access to the garden does not come through the blood of David's mighty men, but only through the blood of David's Son, an even mightier Man. By pouring out the water, David acknowledged that the final redemption had not yet occurred. The water could not yet come from Bethlehem because Jesus was not yet glorified.[5]

When the chips were down and the odds were stacked against us, when the enemy had the strategic advantage and we languished in the valley, our great Mighty Man broke through the enemy lines and drew water for us. At great risk, enormous cost to himself, he procured water from the well of salvation, he saved us from death, we drink his blood, quench our spiritual thirst, live because he died.

---

5. Leithart, *Son to Me*, 314.

12

David
Burying the Benjamin Problem

And they buried the bones of Saul and his son Jonathan in the land of
Benjamin in Zela, in the tomb of Kish his father. And they did all that the
king commanded. And after that God responded to the plea for the land.

—2 SAMUEL 21:14

PEACE-MAKING IS A NON-NEGOTIABLE Christian calling. It was a significant
part of David's vocation, often missed by a readership that takes peace for
granted. For those for whom war, tribalism and revenge are part of reality,
striving for peace is integral to Christian mission. For many Bethlehem
Christians, this is front and centre of their witness.

Shireen Awad Hilal, who was born and raised in Beit Shahour—the
Shepherd's Fields—and who is currently Dean of Students and an Instruc-
tor at Bethlehem Bible College, includes "peacemaker" in her vocabulary of
identity, "What does it mean for me to be a Palestinian Christian woman

who is a peacemaker? Peace is not passive. And peace is not silent. Peace protests. Peace acts. And peace disrupts the status quo."[1]

According to Munther Isaac, there are two New Testament verses that speak about being children of God: John 1:12, where those who *believe* become children of God, and Matthew 5:9, where those who *make peace* are called children of God. He marvels that Evangelical Christians put disproportionate weight on the former, often neglecting the latter.

> This separation of action from belief is an easy one to make today, freeing us Christians from our responsibility to work for peace and justice in our world. We need to teach the whole truth about Jesus and look at his ministry holistically, emphasizing this teaching that you become a child of God when you are a peacemaker.[2]

THE ROOTS OF RECONCILIATION

David will spend a huge amount of leadership time, energy and resource trying to heal the ancient, toxic rift between Judah and Benjamin, the sons of Leah and the sons of Rachel. Reconciliation is a major part of his mission. The roots of reconciliation are there in David's bloodline, and in the geography of Bethlehem. According to Yael Ziegler,

> The story of Ruth contains within it the potential to mend the rift between Rachel and Leah . . . Bethlehem (and Ephrath) is an apt place to symbolize the merger of the two houses. After all, it is both part of the inheritance of the children of Leah and associated with Rachel's burial. It is not surprising, therefore, that kingship, which was conceived in order to draw these factions together, emerges from this place of unification."[3]

When Saul vs David descends into a civil war—Benjamin vs Judah—David's goal is not victory but reconciliation. In a Middle Eastern tribal context, where memories are weapons and every slight on honour is nursed and tallied for an equal and opposite revenge, David finds new ways of moving toward "the other," of refusing retaliation, of building peace. This peace-making messianic emphasis is developed by the prophets. For example, Isaiah looks forward to a Prince of Peace (Is 9:6), and to a Seed

---

1. Hilal, "Peacemakers."
2. Isaac, *The Other Side,* 173.
3. Ziegler, *Ruth,* 438–9.

of Jesse who will cause the wolf to lay down with the lamb (Is 11:6). The greater David will create peace between God and man, and love between enemies. To what extent will the first David succeed in his attempt to bury the Benjamin problem?

FRIENDSHIP: JONATHAN AND MICHAL

The half-siblings Jonathan and Michal, both of whom were children of Saul, represent David's first attempt at love for enemies. Their stories are similar in many ways.

Jonathan loved David, and vowed to hand over his father's kingdom to David (1 Sam 18:3-4). This represented a significant betrayal of his father, his family and his tribe, drawing in due course a hate-filled public shaming and assassination attempt by his father (1 Sam 20:30-34).[4] And yet Jonathan never fully went over to David. He remained in the palace not the wilderness. He was caught between loyalty and love, between past and future, between two irreconcilable gravities, and he died fighting alongside his father.

Michal, we are told, also loved David (1 Sam 18:20). Her father was seeking a political alliance through marriage, but it backfired when Michal started machinating *for* David and *against* Saul (1 Sam 18:28-29). This may be the only example of a Benjamin-Judah marriage in the Bible, and it was not a happy one. Michal, like Jonathan, struggled her whole life between these two allegiances. The narrator demonstrates this by sometimes calling her "David's wife" and at other times, "Saul's daughter." In 1 Samuel 19 and 20, both Jonathan and Michal helped David escape from their father by deceiving him. And both came to sad endings. Jonathan died on Gilboa, and Michal exited the story when she complained that David was not acting in king-like fashion. In this passage, she is referred to as "daughter of Saul" three times, and her final verse writes her out of the story forever:

> And Michal the daughter of Saul had no child to the day of her death. 2 Samuel 6:23

This first reconciliation attempt, through the love of Saul's children for David (whose name means "Beloved") came to an abortive end. Michal

---

4. This passage expresses a conflict which I have seen many Muslim background believers experience in their own wrestling between family and faith.

never bore a half Judahite-half Benjaminite child to unite the tribes, and both exited the story sadly. This animosity would take a long time to kill.

HEBRON: ABNER SIGNS A PEACE

After the deaths of Saul and Jonathan, civil war proper broke out. David, in Hebron, led the tribe of Judah, and his three cousins, the sons of Zeruiah, Joab, Abishai, and Asahel, were key captains in his army. On the other side, Saul's son Ish-bosheth was announced king over the northern tribes, and his uncle Abner led his fighting men. Abner, the old, grizzled, experienced general, seems to have held the real power in Benjamin.

Following the bloody battle of Gibeon, Abner fled and Asahel, young and swift, pursued him on foot. The text of 2 Samuel 2:18–23 shows that Abner repeatedly warned Asahel, and tried to resist killing him, but in the end reversed his spear into the stomach of his pursuer, and Asahel bled out from the stomach wound and died.

Joab did what any honour-loving Middle Eastern big brother would do, nursed a grudge and waited for the opportunity to avenge his brother. Eye for eye, tooth for tooth, life for life. Honour tainted must be re-claimed.

Abner, perhaps seeing that they were losing the war, perhaps because of his falling-out with Ish-bosheth, decided to defect to David and sue for peace. Abner and the delegation with him travelled to David in Hebron, signed a historic peace deal between Judah and Benjamin, making David king over all Israel, and was sent away "in peace."

At that moment Joab, returning from a raid, was told that his brother's killer had been and gone, and that the king had "sent him away, and he had gone in peace." Joab, in his anger and thirst for revenge, sent messengers after Abner to call him back under false pretences, met him in the gate of Hebron, and "there he stuck him in the stomach, so that he died, for the blood of Asahel his brother" (1 Sam 3:29). He claimed his right of satisfaction. The perfect vengeance, stomach-wound for stomach-wound.

Hebron had been designated a city of refuge, and a man seeking asylum from the family avenger could shelter in its gate and appeal for forgiveness. Yet here, in the very gate supposed to symbolise forgiveness, Joab avenged his brother.

David was determined to distance himself from any responsibility for Abner's death, under the flag of truce, which he demonstrated by cursing Joab, giving Abner an honourable burial, and mourning him publicly. All of this is counter-cultural, to curse a cousin and mourn an enemy, to deny a man the right of family vengeance, to give a state funeral to an ancient enemy and persecutor. The people would have been shocked, offended, even ashamed by these actions—to honour one of *them* and humiliate one of *us*? David, who had publicly mourned Saul and Jonathan, now mourned Abner. He was determined to bury enmity at all costs. He understood that the cycle of vengeance has no end, blood begets blood, and that the only way to create peace is by someone *not* restoring honour, through absorption of the honour-cost, and burial and mourning of an enemy.

The oft-heard Arab proverb, "I and my brothers against my cousins; I and my cousins against my tribe; I and my tribe against the world,"[5] is here inverted and superseded by the king, who is redefining identity and belonging, loyalty and peace, honour and vengeance.

MEPHIBOSHETH COVERED

David, determined to fulfil his covenanted obligation of kindness (*khesed*) to Jonathan, enquired whether he had any surviving relatives, and discovered one surviving son. Mephibosheth, meaning "From the Mouth of Shame,"[6] was discovered in hiding across the Jordan amongst Saul sympathisers in a place called Lo-debar, meaning "Nothing." Mephibosheth was deep in shame for so many reasons, his name, his defeated family, and most of all, his crippled feet. Disability in that context, at that time, implied embarrassment, powerlessness, a bad fate—ideas which tragically and unfortunately still have currency in some places today. Just to be clear, a Christian view of the world does not place shame upon disability in any way whatsoever.

Mephibosheth was invited to Jerusalem to take a place, amongst the king's sons, at the king's table. This, the highest of honours, covered Mephibosheth's shame, just as the table would have covered the lameness of his feet. Covering, deriving from the root *kpr,* is the origin of the word for atonement.[7] Atonement is a covering of disgrace. Mephibosheth, undeserving as he was, had his shame atoned for by a gracious intervention of David. David showed a *khesed* that could never be reciprocated to a former enemy. His patronage put Mephibosheth in his debt, produced in him loyalty and gratitude. Mephibosheth became part of David's household.

5. Musk, *Touching the Soul of Islam,* 156.

6. Saul's son Ish-bosheth has a name meaning *Man of Shame.*

7. E.g. *Yom Kippur,* the Day of Atonement.

Showing grace to enemies is a staggering pre-figuring of the gospel, a way of building peace. In this action, we glimpse the cross, as Christ welcomes us, his enemies, to his table, covering our shame in an act of extraordinary grace (Rom 5:10). Like Rahab, far off to near, shame to honour, enemy to family, the hospitality of God (Eph 2:13–19).

SHIMEI: CURSING LEFT UNANSWERED

During Absalom's coup, David and his household fled Jerusalem eastwards, down towards the Jordan, the direction of exile. As they traipsed wearily into the Judean wilderness, Shimei, a relative of Saul, began cursing the king and showering him with stones (2 Sam 16:5–13). This humiliation should never have gone unanswered. Abishai, ever keen to defend the king's honour, asked permission to go and "take off his head" (2 Sam 16:9). David's response, again counter-cultural, was to turn the other cheek. The lion of Judah chose a lamb-response.

> It may be that the LORD will look on the wrong done to me, and that the LORD will repay me with good for his cursing today." 2 Samuel 16:12

This extraordinary response, a non-retaliative absorption of insults, is alien to an honour-shame world, where slights to honour must be repaid. This meekness is seen as weakness. And yet, David's forbearance was vindicated. On his return to the throne after Absalom's brief coup, as his retinue prepared to re-cross the Jordan, they were met by a repentant Shimei, and with him a thousand Benjamites, a whole pack of wolves, coming to bow the knee (19:16–23). Once again, David proves that forgiveness has the power to win over enemies, and that absorption of insults breaks the cycle of vengeance. David was working hard, at great personal cost, to create peace with Benjamin.

BURYING OLD BONES

A final example of David's determination to end the animosity between Judah and Benjamin can be seen in 2 Samuel 21. After a three-year drought, David, seeking the Lord, resolved to rediscover Saul and Jonathan's unburied bones and give them an honourable burial.

> David went and took the bones of Saul and the bones of his son
> Jonathan from the men of Jabesh-gilead, who had stolen them
> from the public square of Beth-shan, where the Philistines had
> hanged them, on the day the Philistines killed Saul on Gilboa. And
> he brought up from there the bones of Saul and the bones of his
> son Jonathan; and they gathered the bones of those who were
> hanged. And they buried the bones of Saul and his son Jonathan
> in the land of Benjamin in Zela, in the tomb of Kish his father.
> And they did all that the king commanded. And after that God
> responded to the plea for the land. 2 Samuel 21:12–14

Death by hanging was considered a way of cursing, and failure to bury
the corpses meant that the curse persisted (Deut 21:22, 23). Only burying
the body could stop the malediction. This final action of David, giving his
enemies honourable burial in their own family tomb in their own tribal
lands, appears finally to have put the unrest to rest, ended the drought,
zeroed all outstanding balances, and buried the Benjamin problem.

Christ also was hung, considered cursed, and buried to remove the
curse of sin and death from the world. His burial is the cleansing of the
earth from the curse, the zeroing of all balances, the introduction of rest.

In David we observe a persistence in peace-making, employing a va-
riety of strategies over decades of his life, a single-minded determination
to tear down the wall of hostility between Judah and Benjamin. And within
his lifespan, he succeeded, even if, a generation after his death, the nation
would once again split along tribal fault-lines.

This determination to kill enmity and create peace is a pre-figuration
of Christ, the Prince of Peace, the Demolisher of Walls, the Killer of Hostility, the Uniter of Brothers.

> But now in Christ Jesus you who once were far off have been
> brought near by the blood of Christ. For he himself is our peace,
> who has made us both one and has broken down in his flesh the
> dividing wall of hostility by abolishing the law of commandments
> expressed in ordinances, that he might create in himself one new
> man in place of the two, so making peace, and might reconcile us
> both to God in one body through the cross, thereby killing the
> hostility. Ephesians 2:13–16

When one looks at the "security wall" surrounding Bethlehem, separating communities, one sees a tangible example of the very thing Christ
came to tear down. Munther Isaac explains how physical walls exacerbate
mistrust and hatred:

Walls communicate fear and shape perceptions of the "other." They prevent the ordinary people of both sides from meeting one another, and as such, images are created of the other—often false and negative ones. Walls convey the message that those behind the wall are to be feared and not to be trusted. They insist that the ordinary people of both sides of the divide cannot co-exist. This is a false premise that must be rejected and challenged.[8]

How does the cross of Jesus Christ bring down walls? At the cross, many of the radical peacebuilding strategies of David find their ultimate fulfilment in the death of Jesus Christ. Volf explains:

The cross breaks the cycle of violence. Hanging on the cross, Jesus provided the ultimate example of his command to replace the principle of retaliation ("an eye for an eye and a tooth for a tooth") with the principle of nonresistance ("if anyone strikes you on the right cheek, turn the other also") (Matthew 5:38–43). By suffering violence as an innocent victim, he took upon himself the aggression of the persecutors. He broke the vicious cycle of violence by absorbing it, taking it upon himself. He refused to be sucked into the automatism of revenge, but sought to overcome evil by doing good—even at the cost of his life.[9]

Blessed are the peacemakers, for they will be called sons of God (Matt 5:9). Jesus, the Son of God, is the great Maker of Peace.

8. Isaac, *The Other Side,* 106.

9. Volf, *Exclusion and Embrace,* 292.

13

David
O, Jerusalem, Jerusalem!

> Nevertheless, David took the stronghold of Zion, that is, the city of David.
>
> —2 SAMUEL 5:7

JERUSALEM. A SMALL, CRAGGY fortress perched atop a rock. It was less a city at this point than a mountain stronghold with a tiny population. With only one natural spring, Jerusalem would always struggle to maintain a sizeable settlement. Most conquerors of Palestine would bypass it completely, extracting payment in lieu of siege;[1] the rewards were not worth the arduous investment of time and resources required to besiege it. Yet David is determined to make Jerusalem his new capital.

This is a politically astute move. Joshua failed to conquer Jerusalem. David, in taking the city, shows that he is greater than Joshua. More importantly, Jerusalem is in the territory of Benjamin, right on the border, in fact, between Judah and Benjamin (Josh 8:28). As long as he was in Hebron, David could only really be king of Judah, reinforcing tribal loyalties for and

---

1. Shishaq, King of Egypt, Hazael, King of Damascus, and Sennacherib, King of Assyria. Halpern, *David's Secret Demons*, 318.

against his reign. But now that the war is over, David can be magnanimous in victory and centre his united kingdom in Benjamin.

In many ways, 2 Samuel 5–8 is the climax of the whole journey out of Egypt, into the promised land, and now, finally, the ark of God and the people of God can rest. The bringing up of the ark in chapter 6 is a key moment. In this account, "ark" is used fifteen times, of which seven are "ark of God" and seven others "ark of the Lord"—a double seven for a sabbatical theme: at the end of battles and labours the Lord is giving rest, and sacred space is being consecrated.[2] This moment is also a victorious reversal of the loss of the ark in 1 Samuel 4:10–11, where thirty thousand men of Israel fell. In 2 Samuel 6:1, David assembles thirty thousand men of Israel for the celebration. Defeat turned into victory, death into strength, exile into homecoming.

Second Samuel 7 is the longest monologue of God since Sinai. Zion, the latest mountain-top home of God, will be a new Sinai, a new Eden. In this speech, "house" is mentioned seven times, the sabbatical idea of rest is reinforced. Many of the Bethlehem themes are reiterated, leadership as shepherding the flock, *khesed*, the Seed coming from David's own body. It would be forgivable to assume that Bethlehem has been bettered by Jerusalem, that God at the centre has replaced God at the margins, that religious and political alignment was the goal all along, but in the unravelling to come, it is clear that this is not the case. At best, there is a temporary convergence between the purposes of God and the narrative of political power in David, but it is very brief, and followed soon afterwards by a dramatic divergence.

Even a careful reading of 2 Samuel 7 will yield this conclusion. Consider the Seed-promise in verses 12 to 14:

> When your days are fulfilled and you lie down with your fathers, I will raise up your offspring [seed] after you, who shall come from your body, and I will establish his kingdom. He shall build a house for my name, and I will establish the throne of his kingdom forever. I will be to him a father, and he shall be to me a son. 2 Samuel 7:12–14

These promises point in part, but only in part, to David's heir Solomon. Solomon was David's fourth son, the first three having disqualified themselves, much as Jacob's fourth son Judah became his heir after the oldest three had disqualified themselves. Solomon would build the great

2. Leithart, *Son to Me*, 210.

Jerusalem temple. But he would never be known as God's son. And his kingdom would not last forever. No, these words would only be fulfilled much, much later by the Seed of David, the Son of God, who would build a dwelling-place for the Spirit throughout the earth, not in Jerusalem, and sit an eternal throne. Jesus, who, like David, was born in Bethlehem and died in Jerusalem, is the one who stood in the city a few days before his death *at its hands*, declaring,

> "O Jerusalem, Jerusalem, the city that kills the prophets and stones those who are sent to it!" Matthew 23:37

Jerusalem is death to prophets. Power kills the impulse of the Spirit. This is crystal clear in David's story. When David, the Bethlehem shepherd with wilderness in his soul, goes up to Jerusalem, his entire story begins to unravel.

THE UNRAVELLING

Jerusalem is a turning point in David's life, and in the story of Israel, but the point is, it is not a positive one. We sense the danger in the final words of chapter 8, where we read that "David's sons were priests" (2 Sam 8:18). Why is David seeking to concentrate civil and religious power in his family? Later, King Jehoiakim executes the prophet Uriah (Jer 26:20–23). Much later, King Joash orders the prophet Zechariah to be stoned to death inside the Jerusalem temple (2 Chron 24:21). Herod would appoint his own son-in-law Aristobulus the Younger High Priest in his newly-constructed temple. Many of the horrors perpetrated in the name of religion have derived from this impulse, the impulse of kings to bring the worship of God under their purview.

It should not surprise us that, now Israel is in the land and at rest, sin should follow. As soon as creation was prepared, Adam sinned in the garden. The shiny new beginning through Noah was immediately tarnished. And now David, like a new Adam, is dwelling in the land, it is time for sin's discordant anti-climax to shatter the illusory peace. Make no mistake, there are no happy endings until Christ comes.

The Bathsheba story reads like Genesis 3, Bathsheba is the forbidden fruit which David "saw" was "good" and "took" (Gen 3:6; 2 Sam 11:2–4). The consequences include David's exile from the land eastwards, like Adam, and repercussions which echo through his family, including sons who kill each other, like Adam's son Cain killed Abel.

> When David's children re-enact his crimes as part of his punish-ment, David's adultery with Bathsheba is replayed as rape, not once but twice. Following closely upon this scene, Amnon rapes his sister Tamar (2 Sam. 13), who, like Bathsheba, is beautiful (13:1) and, like Bathsheba, is objectified (13:17). And when Absa-lom does in the sight of the sun and all Israel what David had done in secret, he openly rapes ten of David's wives in a tent pitched for him on the roof—the roof, of course, serving as a reminder that this is where David's crime began (2 Sam. 12:11–12; 16:21–22).[3]

The Bathsheba incident, narrated across two chapters, is bookended with explicit reference to Jerusalem (11:1 and 12:31). It happened because, rather than "going out" to lead the army, David was already beginning to be seduced by the lulling, narcoticising effects of wealth and security—the Je-rusalem atmosphere within which Solomon and his son Rehoboam would grow up.[4] David will repent, suffer exile and return, and live to see his fourth son, Solomon, crowned successor, the first three having disqualified themselves. But as the Seed-line is dislocated from its Bethlehem origins, so is it weakened. Kings born in Jerusalem do not save, kings born in Beth-lehem do.

SOLOMON

After 2 Samuel 5:7, the next appearance of the two names Zion and City of David together comes as Solomon prepares to dedicate his temple in 1 Kings 8:1. Zion is often a reference to the mountain of God (temple), and "City of David" the political capital (palace).[5] This combining of temple and palace in one place, bringing the worship of God under state control, is the great innovation of David and Solomon in Jerusalem, and also the great undoing. Now God is under the king's control. God has lost his free-dom. While David more or less held the tension between Bethlehem and Jerusalem, between wilderness-shepherd and city-statesman, between free God and temple-constrained God, he set a trajectory that Solomon and his

---

3. Exum, *Fragmented Women*, Kindle Location 3729.

4. In particular, the scene of the crime is "the king's house." "House" is a leading word across chapters 6–12, occurring some 53 times.

5. Morrison, *2 Samuel*, 75.

descendants would continue. The dilemma is this: Solomon, Israel's mightiest and richest king, was at the same time depicted by Scripture as Pharaoh.

Solomon mirrors Pharaoh in many ways. He initiates forced labour and in particular the building of store cities (1 Kgs 9:19), he is obsessed with horses and chariots, he is depicted as "whipping" the nation (12:14). As Pharaoh treated Israel, so Solomon is treating his own people. Hadad's cameo appearance in 1 Kings 11 paints him remarkably similar to Moses, the implication being that Solomon is now a Pharaoh-tyrant who needs to be resisted.[6] In addition, as Alex Israel notes, the account of Solomon's reign is bookended by his relationship with Pharaoh's daughter:

> In hindsight, the tight intertwining of Solomon with Pharaoh's daughter serves as a grim and deeply troubling refrain in his story. By making their marriage the opening (3:1) and closing (11:1) note of the Solomon narrative, the Bible is tainting Solomon from start to finish.[7]

The mighty scholar Brueggemann's perspective on this narrative flow of the Old Testament is unapologetic: Israel has gone the way of the surrounding nations. In Egypt, God initiated the revolution and brought the oppressed people out. The Hebrews knew God as a free God on the move, God of plague and desert and tent. A free God frees people. But now, with God domiciled next door to the palace, he is at the king's beck and call. Jerusalem is no different from Babylon or Thebes, Solomon is Nimrod and Pharaoh.

> Solomon managed what one would think is not possible, for he had taken the Mosaic innovation and rendered it null and void. In tenth-century Jerusalem it is as though the whole revolution and social experiment had not happened. The long sequence of imperial history went on as though it had not been interrupted by this revelation of the liberating God. Solomon managed a remarkable

---

6. Alex Israel notes, "Both Hadad and Moses are born against the backdrop of the killing of the males of their nations. Saved as a young child, each grows up in Pharaoh's house as royalty. They each escape to Midian and marry the daughter of their protector in the land to which they have fled (Jethro/Pharaoh). And in each case, upon the death of a despotic ruler (Pharaoh/David), they request leave of their father-in-law to return to their oppressed brethren and lead the opposition to the oppressive regime." Israel, *I Kings*, Kindle Location 2907.

7. Israel, *I Kings*, Kindle Location 2784.

continuity with the very Egyptian reality that Moses had sought to counter.[8]

Halpern notes that king and palace together, state-sponsored religion, was an Egyptian idea, and that Solomon was "aping" Egypt. "The Jerusalem establishment, especially in Solomon's day, manifests an Egyptianizing conception of the nature of monarchy . . . the creation of a monumental capital city and of a huge temple in the backyard of the royal palace both project an image that apes Egyptian models."[9]

Remember, God did not seem to want Israel to have a king, just as he did not want to live in a temple (2 Sam 7:5–7). In 1 Samuel 8, when the people asked Samuel for a king, "like all the nations" (v. 5), God told Samuel,

> Obey the voice of the people in all that they say to you, for they have not rejected you, but they have rejected me from being king over them. According to all the deeds that they have done, from the day I brought them up out of Egypt even to this day, forsaking me and serving other gods, so they are also doing to you. Now then, obey their voice; only you shall solemnly warn them and show them the ways of the king who shall reign over them. 1 Samuel 8:7–9

The prophet then warned the people at length about the trouble that having a king "like the other nations" would bring on the nation (v. 10–18). This list of warnings was fulfilled word for word in the litany of Solomon's exploits (1 Kings 11). Likewise, Solomon's list of sins in 1 Kings 11 directly reflects Moses' warning about kings in Deuteronomy 17:14–20. It really is remarkable how briefly the united kingdom, centred in Jerusalem, existed. One generation. And Solomon's temple, built with such care at the beginning of 1 Kings, is destroyed by Nebuchadnezzar at the end of 2 Kings. Herod's temple, built later, would also last only a short time before being destroyed by Rome. Jerusalem temples do not have great life expectancy.

It is important that this perspective be captured. As soon as David peaks, he unravels. He is able, remarkable man that he is, to repent and re-align himself with God, but his sons, beginning with Solomon, are not able to hold this tension. God is angry with Solomon, and takes away the kingdom (1 Kgs 11:9). The enormous prosperity and progress that characterise

---

8. Brueggemann, *Prophetic Imagination,* Kindle Location 982.

9. Halpern, *David's Secret Demons,* 291.

Solomon's reign, supported by archaeology,[10] are not a mark of God's presence, but a harbinger of his absence. Power corrupts, wealth leads astray, and satiation deadens the prophetic impulse. From now on, God is present with the marginal prophets who butt heads with kings. "This tradition of royal authoritarianism and of poetic (prophetic) interruption is a rivalry that permeates Israel's tradition," writes Brueggemann.[11] Muilenburg is also explicit that the prophets are anti-power: "One of the most striking and one of the most pervasive features of the prophetic polemic [is] the denunciation and distrust of power in all its forms and guises."[12]

Suspicion of power is not a twenty-first century innovation. It is as old as the prophets. It is a key feature of the story that it unravels as soon as it peaks. Otherwise we have a Hollywood rags-to-riches tale, from the pasture to the palace, that glorifies wealth and power as the ultimate goal. Humble beginnings are despised if superseded, Bethlehem forgotten in the shadow of Jerusalem. The idols of wealth and comfort and power roar so loudly in our ears, sparkle so attractively in our eyes, that we fail to see the dangers posed by Jerusalem to the dynamic life of the people of God.

Of course, there are many, many positive threads concerning Jerusalem running through Scripture. From its first mention in association with Melchizedek (Gen 14:18) to John's vision of the New Jerusalem (Rev 21:2), a longing for the ideal city of God is indeed in evidence. A temple atop Mount Zion is the fulfilment of multiple themes tracing their roots, ultimately, to Eden. Eden was high ground, facing East, with rivers flowing out of it (Gen 2:8–10, Ez 28:13–14). Eden was the first temple, Adam the first priest.[13] Solomon's temple was also atop a mountain, facing East. The engravings of fruit, the cherubim guarding the sanctuary, Ezekiel's vision of a river flowing eastwards (Ez 47:1) all recall Eden. Zion is the ideal sanctuary, the dwelling of God.[14]

In the Psalms, intense desire and longing is expressed for this perfect dwelling of God amongst his people; "Glorious things of you are spoken, O city of God."[15] In the prophets, a yearning for the prosperity of Jerusalem

---

10. Brueggemann, *Prophetic Imagination,* Kindle Location 908.

11. Brueggemann, *Interrupting Silence,* 27.

12. Muilenburg, *The Way of Israel,* 89.

13. Beale, *A New Testament Biblical Theology,* 617.

14. Eden means "delight." Psalm 36:8 makes another connection between Zion and Eden; "You give them drink from the river of your delights (*edens*)."

15. Psalm 87:3.

is articulated again and again. A clear vision of a harmonious community, indwelt by God himself, demonstrating justice and righteousness emerges. And yet, this vision is never fulfilled in the physical city of Jerusalem. Just as Ezekiel's vision of a great river flowing from the city is prophetic, eschatological, never literally fulfilled, so too Isaiah's vision of death being swallowed up forever on Zion (Is 25:8), and the Psalmist's claim that even Gentiles will be included in the city register; "the Lord records as he registers the peoples, 'This one was born there.'"[16] Throughout the Old Testament, this longing for the ideal sanctuary and perfect multi-ethnic city, or polis, is concentrated on Jerusalem, but always unattainable, out of reach, unrealised. The continued reality of sin prohibits perfection.

Until Jesus. With Jesus, the dwelling of God is centred in a person, not a place (John 1:14, 2:21). With Jesus, the temple is constructed from living stones spread across the world (1 Cor 6:19, 1 Pet 2:4–7). With Jesus, the Reality has come, and types and shadows pass away (Heb 10:1). With Jesus, faith's focus shifts therefore from an earthly Jerusalem to a heavenly one (Gal 4:26, Heb 12:22). With Jesus, a new creation is set in motion, culminating with John's vision of "the holy city, the new Jerusalem, coming down out of heaven from God, prepared as a bride adorned for her husband."[17] A Christian reading of the whole story of Scripture directs one's yearning and desire not to a temporal Jerusalem but to an eternal one, not to a national community but to a global one, not to a political capital but to a spiritual one. All of the Old Testament ache for Zion is gathered up, summed up and tied up in Jesus himself, and in His body, the church.

Both positive and negative aspects of Jerusalem run through the Bible, the aspirational and the unachievable. The brief convergence of the Seed storyline and Jerusalem is not a happy one, and almost immediately the prophets begin to call for a re-divergence. There are no happy endings without Jesus. And Jesus comes from Bethlehem.

MISSION AND PROPHECY

Mission and prophecy are similar in many ways. Both pull away from the centre. Both find life in the margins. Both begin with lament and express an element of protest. Both are predicated on the freedom of God. Mission and prophecy are both anti-establishment, both seek creative expression in

16. Psalm 87:6.

17. Rev 21:2.

order to live, both argue that God can best be expressed, best be found, not in centres of power, but amongst the unexpected and unlikely. Both seek to disempower power. Both are enemies of settled-ness, comfort, and control. State-sponsored mission is imperialism, and state-sponsored prophecy is propaganda.

Mission is at its best when it is prophetic. Prophecy is at its best when it is missional. And when mission and prophecy combine, they are potent indeed! Bethlehem is both a missional paradigm and a prophetic paradigm. The truths we learn from the Bethlehem story will help us perceive prophetically and live missionally.

A significant learning from David's ascension to Jerusalem is this: Jerusalem kills prophets. Power and prophecy cannot co-habit. God does not want to live in a temple built by human hands, at the beck and call of kings.

This was a key theme of the late Cragg, that this same Jerusalem, even today with her complicated and painful politics, is still emblematic of religion's misplaced quest for power. In the crowded bazaars of the old city, three religions jostle for ownership. Over the centuries Christendom—the Crusades being its most ugly manifestation—Islam, and now Zionism have all pursued "the same policy of forceful acquisition on the principle that unless we enthrone we cannot pray."[18] Cragg's argument with Islam, Zionism and Christendom is precisely that the Constantinising tendency always corrupts. "Any Constantine will likely be self-serving in the more vigorously serving the Church. So tragically proved to be the case when he turned a Christianity into a Christendom."[19]

None of these are the religion of Messiah, the Christ who rules with wounded hands, the shepherd of Bethlehem. Christ attains his throne not by butchering opponents but by being butchered, not by shedding blood on the Temple Mount but by sweating blood at Gethsemane. He enters Jerusalem not on a war horse, like Simon the Maccabee a century earlier, but on a donkey, because in times of war kings ride horses, but in times of peace, kings ride donkeys (Zech 9:9–10). Jesus did not come to Jerusalem to start a war, but to start a peace. Pentecost is the ultimate challenge to Solomon and Herod's temple-building, where the dwelling of God becomes multi-lingual, multi-centric, and not contingent on Jerusalem.

18. Cragg, *Wounded Hands,* note to cover design.

19. Cragg, *Wounded Hands,* 89.

14

Rehoboam
You Can't Weaponise Bethlehem

He made the fortresses strong, and put commanders in them, and stores of
food, oil, and wine.

And he put shields and spears in all the cities and made them very
strong. So he held Judah and Benjamin.

—2 CHRONICLES 11:11–12

UP THE HILL TO Bethlehem come Rehoboam's workmen, to turn the village into a fortress. Solomon's son Rehoboam inherited the throne with the
odds stacked against him. Egypt's punitive force was on its way northwards,
and as a defensive strategy he fortified Judah's towns, forming a shield
around Jerusalem—including turning his ancestral village, Bethlehem,
into a castle. Quiet villages slumbering among the olive groves became
military garrisons overnight. Rehoboam was wrong. God himself was supposed to be Israel's shield and protector. Rehoboam's reliance on "strength"
was proven false in two ways. Firstly, relative to Egypt, it was no strength
at all, as Pharaoh Sheshonq (whom the Bible calls Shishak) demonstrated
by razing these cities to the ground with ease. Secondly, true strength is

found in trusting the Lord, as Isaiah would tell a later king (Is 30:15), and as was proved when Rehoboam repented and Jerusalem was spared, albeit humiliated.

SOLOMON AND JEROBOAM

The Bible is explicit in blaming Solomon for the dismemberment of the kingdom. David's great unifying project really did not last very long. Once the Seed was allied with power, the voice of the prophets turned against him.

> Therefore the LORD said to Solomon, "Since this has been your practice and you have not kept my covenant and my statutes that I have commanded you, I will surely tear the kingdom from you and will give it to your servant.
>
> Yet for the sake of David your father I will not do it in your days, but I will tear it out of the hand of your son.
>
> However, I will not tear away all the kingdom, but I will give one tribe to your son, for the sake of David my servant and for the sake of Jerusalem that I have chosen." 1 Kings 11:11–13

As he had consistently done, God turned away from the centre and chose a small, insignificant man from the margins. Jeroboam, from the hill country of Ephraim, son of a widow, working on the walls of the city—unassuming, unlikely, unthreatening. The prophet Ahijah apprehended him with a crystal clear prophecy: when Solomon is dead and his son reigns, I will give you ten tribes and leave one tribe for Rehoboam. If you prove yourself godly, I will give you a great dynasty. "And," says the Lord, "I will afflict the offspring of David because of this, yet not forever" (1 Kgs 11:26–40). When Solomon's secret police brought him news of this, he sought to eliminate the threat—a very Pharaoh-Saul-Herod thing to do. The Seed is acting like the Snake. Jeroboam fled to Egypt to seek the patronage of Pharaoh Sheshonq, and to wait for Solomon to die (1 Kgs 11:40).

Solomon died in 931 BC, and Rehoboam became king, with threats to his rule all around. He knew that Jeroboam would be back, with the promise of God in his heart and the sponsorship of mighty Pharaoh. During the time of Solomon, Egypt had not been a threat—Solomon's marriage to one of Pharaoh's daughters had secured an uneasy alliance.

Rehoboam, named after his ancestress Rahab, had a name meaning "Broad Land." Born and named when Solomon's kingdom was at its greatest extent, his name became painfully ironic as the kingdom split on his watch.

MINORITISATION LEADS TO ALIENATION

Jeroboam, as expected, returned to lead the north in rebellion, predicated on the unjust labour and taxation policies of Rehoboam (12:2). Egyptian pastor-scholar Youssef Samir, who spends twelve pages decrying Rehoboam's dictatorship in his article *The Cross and the Power Issue: A Middle Eastern View,* writes:

> Perhaps the main reason behind this feeling of those who suffer under any dictatorial rule is that they sense they do not belong to the country, the institution, or the family in which they live: rather, they are exposed to strong and injuring humiliation, underappreciation, and absence of equality, which all entail the denial of community belonging. . . . He chose to be the cold-hearted master, so they chose to be indifferent slaves.[1]

Minoritisation and injustice leads to alienation. The north splits along ancient tribal fault-lines (at Shechem, where Joseph was attacked by his half-brothers, a place steeped in Leah-Rachel antagonism), and Rehoboam is suddenly left with a tiny kingdom, vulnerable to attack from the north and from Egypt to the south. He decides to dig in. He fortifies a double ring of defensive towns around Jerusalem.

> Rehoboam lived in Jerusalem, and he built cities for defence in Judah.
> He built Bethlehem, Etam, Tekoa,
> Beth-zur, Soco, Adullam,
> Gath, Mareshah, Ziph,
> Adoraim, Lachish, Azekah,
> Zorah, Aijalon, and Hebron, fortified cities that are in Judah and in Benjamin.
> He made the fortresses strong, and put commanders in them, and stores of food, oil, and wine.
> And he put shields and spears in all the cities and made them very strong. So he held Judah and Benjamin. 2 Chronicles 11:5–12

1. Samir, "The Cross and the Power Issue," 390.

REHOBOAM'S DEFENSIVE STRATEGY

Jerusalem is positionally defensible, but her weakness under siege has always been the water supply. A large population, including refugees from the surrounding countryside, cannot last long on the supply of the one spring and the collected winter rains in pots and cisterns.

Solomon was a great builder, and he had invested considerable resources in Jerusalem's water infrastructure. Firstly, he had beefed up Jerusalem's external water supply, creating the three large pools southwest of Bethlehem (Eccl 2:4–6) and initiating the first aqueduct bringing water from these pools into Jerusalem, an aqueduct later developed with Roman technology by Pontius Pilate, and still in evidence today.[2]

Secondly, Jerusalem's internal water storage was enhanced when Solomon carved great cisterns underneath the temple complex, necessitated by the need for large quantities of water in the sacrificial ritual. These cisterns would have held run-off from the winter rains and positioned Jerusalem favourably to endure siege.[3] All of this technology would have made Rehoboam feel more confident in preparing to withstand Sheshonq. Technology can enforce the lie of invincibility.

STRENGTH

The Chronicler is very clear that Rehoboam's presumed strength led to his downfall—he trusted in himself and not in God.

> When the rule of Rehoboam was established and he was strong, he abandoned the law of the LORD, and all Israel with him. 2 Chronicles 12:1

This word for "strong" (*chzq*) appears five times in this story (11:11, 12, 17; 12:1, 13). How is it that Rehoboam's strength led to his downfall? Because he looked to himself, not to the Lord, for strength. This is contrasted

---

2. "Whether any part of it [the aqueduct] goes back to Solomon's time, as it is claimed, is more than doubtful. It is the custom in the East to associate any great work with the name of Solomon; hence we get 'Solomon's Pools,' 'Solomon's Quarries,' 'Solomon's Stables,' etc – he is the country's ideal of wisdom and greatness." Masterman, "The Water Supply of Jerusalem," 105.

3. Masterman, "The Water Supply of Jerusalem," 97.

with his grandfather David, who knew what is was to "strengthen (*chzq*) himself in the Lord his God."[4] In Psalm 35, David wrote,

> Contend, O LORD, with those who contend with me; fight against those who fight against me!
> Take hold of [*chzq*] shield and buckler and rise for my help! Psalm 35:1–2

Amos chapter 6, which begins "Woe to those at ease in Zion," decries the self-reliance of a Jerusalem king, especially in verse 8, "I abhor the pride of Jacob and hate his strongholds," and verse 13, when the people say, "have we not by our own strength (*chzq*) captured Karnaim for ourselves?" Strength-reliance is never OK for the people of God.

The second leading word in the Rehoboam story, which, like *chzq* also occurs five times, is *mtsurah*, translated "fortified cities," or "fortresses" (11:5, 10, 11, 23; 12:4). Once again, this is a divergence from David, who believed that God was his fortress.

> In you, O LORD, do I take refuge; let me never be put to shame; in your righteousness deliver me!
> Incline your ear to me; rescue me speedily! Be a rock of refuge for me, a strong fortress [*mtsd*] to save me!
> For you are my rock and my fortress [*mtsd*]; and for your name's sake you lead me and guide me; Psalm 31:1–3

Again, a later prophet would make it plain that fortifying Judah's cities is idolatry:[5]

> For Israel has forgotten his Maker and built palaces, and Judah has multiplied fortified cities; so I will send a fire upon his cities, and it shall devour her strongholds. Hosea 8:14

Contemporary Israeli commentator Alex Israel makes the point that, although in Kings, Rehoboam's sin is called out as idolatry, Chronicles is more subtle. Subtle, yet damning.

> In Chronicles, however, the sin is dramatically different; it is broader and less specific. Here, the sin is one of excessive pride, self-reliance accompanied by an abandonment of God. Rehoboam's military fortifications are proven worthless by Shishak, and must be replaced by faith in and reliance upon God. In the

---

4. 1 Samuel 30:6, see also 1 Samuel 23:16; Psalm 147:13.

5. Heschel, *Prophets*, 212.

resultant war, Jerusalem is spared rather than ravished, because the king is highly responsive to a prophet who mentors him to repentance.[6]

The fortified towns, including Bethlehem, in which Rehoboam invested so much hope, are easily taken by Sheshonq's expeditionary force (2 Chr 12:4), and the Egyptian horde surrounds Jerusalem. Bethlehem is under Egyptian control.

> Then Shemaiah the prophet came to Rehoboam and to the princes of Judah, who had gathered at Jerusalem because of Shishak, and said to them, "Thus says the LORD, 'You abandoned me, so I have abandoned you to the hand of Shishak.'" 2 Chronicles 12:5

The prophet's message is simple. "You abandoned me, so I have abandoned you." Your strength led to complacency and presumption.[7] You had all the fortresses you needed, so you didn't need me. The king and those with him respond, humble themselves, re-entrust themselves into God's hand. And Sheshonq spares Jerusalem, collects tribute in lieu of destruction, and continues northwards.

EGYPT'S PERSPECTIVE

In 1799, Napoleon Bonaparte stood in Karnak, by the Nile, with a company of French scholars, deeply impressed with its size and grandeur—the greatest temple area ever constructed. Karnak, on the east side of Thebes, has an entire wall dedicated to the victory of Pharaoh Sheshonq I. This wall details Sheshonq's victorious campaign northwards through Judea, as far as Megiddo.[8] This is the campaign related in 2 Chronicles chapter 12.

Pharaoh Sheshonq I, who ruled from 945–924 BC, was the founder of Egypt's twenty-second dynasty. Sheshonq, taking advantage of Solomon's death in 931 BC, mobilised for a campaign to subdue troublesome Palestine, which Egypt had long considered part of its own empire, and to secure the coastal road, "The Way of the Land of the Philistines," which went due north from Egypt to Phoenicia and Anatolia. In 925, Sheshonq swept through the region. The Karnak inscription puts things into perspective. Egypt, which was already millennia deep in glory, squashed David's dynasty

---

6. Israel, *I Kings*, Kindle Location 4001.

7. Leithart, *1 & 2 Chronicles*, 135. Japhet, *I & II Chronicles*, 676.

8. Keller, *Bible as History*, 225.

which was still in its first century.[9] Judah's beloved capital Jerusalem paid dearly, whilst Sheshonq doesn't even acknowledge Jerusalem in his inscription. As Lemche writes, "Jerusalem is not mentioned at all in Shoshenq's inscription. He was more interested in the coastal plain, with the intention of being able to control the trade that went through this area."[10] Palestine, as Raheb has written, is a land on the periphery: "Contrary to its religious reputation and geographical location, in reality and geo-politically the land lies on the periphery of the Fertile Crescent and is a borderland for diverse empires."[11]

This perspective is important because it makes clear the folly of Rehoboam in trying to compete with a power such as Egypt, and in trying to weaponise Bethlehem. Those Christians who understand themselves to be a minority, at the margins of the world, appreciate the futility, indeed, the presumptuous idolatry underlying Rehoboam's attempt to turn Bethlehem into a fortress. There is certainly meaning in our faith being born, not in one of the superpowers of Egypt or Assyria or Persia, but in the buffer zone in between. Military might and coercive power are not an option for us, sons and daughters of Bethlehem. Christians, so often, are a people caught in between.

You cannot weaponise Bethlehem, it is a gentle shepherds' town. Rather than turning Bethlehem into a fortress, we follow David's claim that the Lord is our fortress. Rather than making strength our objective in church-building and kingdom-building, we understand that the Lord is our strength. Meekness has no defensive strategy. We do not defend our own honour, our own rights. We cannot and should not compete with Egypt.

One of the reasons that the Western church needs to listen to brothers and sisters from minority-Christian contexts in these days is precisely because *they know how to be a minority*. Generations of resistance and persistence in the margins has honed resilience and wisdom sorely lacking in the Western church which, like Rehoboam, grew up with strength as an option and is ill-equipped for post-Christendom minoritisation. Rehoboam surrounded himself with a homogenous group of advisors just like him (1 Kgs 12:8), and sorely needed a prophetic, outsider voice to bring him to repentance. The Western church can't teach the Western church how to thrive post-Christendom. She needs voices from the margins.

9. Merill, *Kingdom of Priests*, 340.

10. Lemche, *Between Theology and History*, 439.

11. Raheb, *Empire*, 51.

Rehoboam forgot that the Seed needs to be buried in order to multiply. He forgot that Judah-leadership is through self-sacrifice, not self-preservation. He forgot that the people of God cannot compete with world powers. He forgot that the Lord is a shield, a fortress, a defender.

Generations later, Rehoboam's descendent Jesus, trapped between the implacable steel of the Roman empire and a howling crowd of his compatriots, would forbid Peter to reach for his sword, and would refuse to defend his own honour to Pilate, as Isaiah had described, "like a lamb that is led to the slaughter, and like a sheep that before its shearers is silent, so he opened not his mouth" (Is 53:7).

Peter, who bore witness to this holy defencelessness, instructs the church to follow the example of Christ.

> For to this you have been called, because Christ also suffered for you, leaving you an example, so that you might follow in his steps. He committed no sin, neither was deceit found in his mouth. When he was reviled, he did not revile in return; when he suffered, he did not threaten, but continued entrusting himself to him who judges justly. 1 Peter 2:21–23

15

Micah
Too Little, Too Late?

But you, O Bethlehem Ephrathah, who are too little to be among the clans of Judah, from you shall come forth for me one who is to be ruler in Israel, whose coming forth is from of old, from ancient days.

Therefore he shall give them up until the time when she who is in labour has given birth; then the rest of his brothers shall return to the people of Israel.

And he shall stand and shepherd his flock in the strength of the LORD, in the majesty of the name of the LORD his God. And they shall dwell secure, for now he shall be great to the ends of the earth.

—MICAH 5:2–4

UP THE HILL TO Bethlehem comes St Paula with her all-female entourage, dusty and weary from their long journey. Paula, laying eyes on Bethlehem for the first time, began in a loud voice to recite Micah 5:2, pausing to expound the meanings of the Hebrew words and apply them to Jesus. "O

House of Bread," she exclaimed, "where the Bread of Heaven was born! O Ephrathah, the Land of Fruit, bearing the fruit of Jesus!"[1]

The year was 385 AD, and Paula, a wealthy Roman widow, was arriving to take up residence in Bethlehem alongside the great scholar Jerome, who was working on his monumental translation of the Bible from Hebrew to Latin, known as the Vulgate. Paula was another mighty woman of God, another mother in the church, associated with the story of Bethlehem. She was attracted by the asceticism and simplicity of life on the edge of the desert, which must have constituted a profound contrast from her previous way of life amongst Rome's bourgeoise. She poured her fortune into the town, not only as a sponsor of Jerome and his work, but also in building and maintaining a guest house and two monasteries. Within ten years, her passion for Bethlehem had bankrupted her.[2]

Paula had a good knowledge of Hebrew, and worked as an editor of some of Jerome's work. This insight into her understanding of Micah 5 demonstrates that there is nothing new in Christians applying this prophecy to the birth of Christ, indeed, Matthew had already made this connection in Matthew 2:6.

The book of Micah appears to be a giant chiasm, a literary form that works from the outside in with the pivot, or hinge, being right in the centre, at Micah 5:2–4. In this way, Micah's small book is a microcosm of the Bible, or even the story of the world, with the turning point being the birth of a ruler in Bethlehem. Micah, like the Bible, starts with judgement, ends with salvation, and pivots on Bethlehem.

Chapters 4 and 5, in the centre of the book, show the locus of salvation and kingship moving away from Jerusalem and towards Bethlehem. There is a divine juxtaposition in play, Zion is shamed as Bethlehem is honoured, Jerusalem is judged while Bethlehem is praised. Consider 4:8:

> And you, O tower of the flock (*Migdal Eder*), hill of the daughter of Zion, to you shall it come, the former dominion shall come, kingship for the daughter of Jerusalem.

Kingship is moving away from Jerusalem—which has become corrupt, unjust, bloated in privilege and arrogance, and against whom judgement is coming—and towards *Migdal Eder*, the fields of Bethlehem, harking back to the death of Rachel.

---

1. O'Brien, "Early Christian Interpretation of Micah 4–5," 62.
2. Blincoe, *Bethlehem*, 85.

Micah was a village boy from Judah, gone up to the city to prophesy against her corrupt elite, the wealthy who were buying up more and more of the agricultural smallholdings, depriving the rural poor of their right to land that had been in their families for generations. As Allen writes, "doubtless he had first-hand knowledge of the sufferings of the rural proletariat and was thus providentially prepared to voice God's own indignation."[3] So when Micah began to prophesy, peppered with plenty of classic David references, that the future shepherd would be born not in Jerusalem but in Bethlehem, it is not difficult to imagine the outrage that would have ensued. He was championing the margins against the centre, the poor against the rich, the rural against the urban elite. It was a call back to basics, back to David's roots, a return to innocence.

We have seen this trope before, in the comparison of Judah and Tamar, and of Achan and Rahab. God resists the proud and gives grace to the humble. This idea of divine juxtaposition is in evidence again between Jerusalem and Bethlehem here. God wants to make the big a bit smaller, and the little a bit greater. Rogerson calls it "a radical rejection of Jerusalem and the existing Davidic dynasty and a completely new start beginning from Bethlehem."[4] For Petrotta, "it is also an affirmation that God can once again work through humble means, as he did with David, and is not dependant on the royal city and household, which has so deteriorated."[5]

Plenty of medieval interpreters saw it this way, too. The façade of the Orvieto cathedral, alternatively called "the Malediction of Jerusalem" or "the Blessing of Bethlehem," shows two cities, with the Divine Will turning away from one and toward the other. At times, to our shame, the Christian tradition has taken this to antisemitic extremes, with Jerusalem wrongly being thought to represent Judaism and Bethlehem betokening Christianity. Religiously-sanctioned violence against Jews has at times resulted from these misrepresentations of divine election and reprobation. Thank goodness the vast majority of interpreters today have rejected this appalling legacy!

Micah was writing within the parameters of the Jewish faith. His prophecy is a metaphor for God's choice of the humble over the proud, the margins over the centre, a return to the Bethlehem ideal. "Micah gathered up all the nostalgia that in people's minds lingered around the throne and

3. Allen, *Joel, Obadiah, Jonah and Micah*, 240.

4. Rogerson, "Micah," 705.

5. Petrotta, "A Closer Look," 50.

bade them look not back but forward to a mighty fulfilment of the best and greatest of their wistful dreams."[6]

Viola Raheb, a Bethlehem-born contemporary biblical scholar and activist, puts it like this: "When Micah named Bethlehem over Jerusalem as the place from which the Messiah would come, he was making a clear religious and political criticism over and against the religious and political establishment of his own people."[7] Her insight, as a woman, as a Bethlehemite, as one who knows what it is to live under occupation, and as an activist for justice, is that Micah's prophetic passion for justice should become ours. It should not surprise us that voices for justice often arise at the margins, from those free from the blind spots of Jerusalem.

Throughout the history of Christianity, there have been many Micah 5 moments, moments when God has seemingly turned his attention away from the centre (Jerusalem) and positioned himself in the margins (Bethlehem). Actually, Addison observes this to be the normal cycle of the Christian movement: "In the renewal and expansion of the church, the breakthroughs always occur on the fringe of ecclesiastical power-never at the centre. In every generation, in some obscure place, God is beginning something new. That's where we need to be."[8]

The church in the increasingly post-Christian Western world faces the temptation to dig in her heels, to fight for her besieged Jerusalems. She cannot imagine the faith without a presence in the halls of cultural power, without a voice in education and the judiciary and politics.

God, however, is untroubled. His attention is on Bethlehem, place of birth, place of new beginnings, marginal space. He will reach for a new shepherd-boy. Micah's words should fill God's people with hope. You may be stripped of your complex and corrupt institutions, with the nations gazing on your nakedness (Micah 4:10–11), but a babe is being born in nakedness, and he will save his people.

This clear juxtapositional trope is present throughout Scripture: proud-humble, centre-margins, powerful-disempowered, rich-poor. Power-sensitive post-colonial narratives are not a modern innovation. They are present in the prophetic Scriptures, and throughout the Bethlehem story. Modern theologies of liberation and postcolonial readings are

---

6. Allen, *Joel, Obadiah, Jonah and Micah*, 347.

7. Raheb, "Reading Micah 5 in Modern Bethlehem," 65.

8. Addison, *Movements that Change the World*, Kindle Location 265.

re-discovering themes that have always been present in the literature of the Bible, and in the heart of God.

Within these verses (Micah 5:2–4) so many of the Bethlehem-related themes that we have been tracking throughout this journey recur. "Who are too little" speaks of marginality and insignificance. "The clans of Judah" references the chosen messianic tribe. "Come forth" recalls 2 Samuel 5:2, and is a Davidic prompt. That this ruler's "coming forth is from of old, from ancient days" probably means that it was prophesied long ago, although some scholars take this as an indication of eternal supernatural origin.[9]

Verse 3's reference to "when she who is in labour has given birth," looks back as far as Genesis 3, re-visiting the important mother-pregnancy-birth theme associated with Bethlehem. Labour is painful and messy and unclean, yet it is central to the process of new life. The Pure One will be born through blood and pain. Verse 4 tells us that this ruler will be a shepherd—*the* shepherd king from Bethlehem. "Stand" here means "endure"—his will be an enduring dynasty, as well as worldwide ("to the ends of the earth"). Verse 5 then tells us that "he will be their peace," picked up later by Paul in Ephesians 2:14, speaking of Christ.

All of these themes are familiar within the Bethlehem story. Looking back from where Micah is standing in history, we recognise that he is in alignment with the messianic thread, stretching back to Genesis 3. Looking forward to the birth of Christ, we know that all of these strands will find their perfect and ultimate fulfilment in him, the Shepherd of Bethlehem.

Matthew, when he portrays Herod's Jewish advisors referring to Micah 5:2 as evidence that the Christ was expected to be born in Bethlehem (Matt 2:5–6), was aware of the Jewish tradition associating these verses with Messiah.[10] Hungarian Jewish scholar Vermes affirms this tradition of interpretation:

> The common Jewish interpretative tradition, represented by the Aramaic *Targum Jonathan to the Prophets*, identifies the 'ruler' with 'the Messiah' (at Micah 5:2; 5:1 in the Hebrew Bible) and the 'Tower of the Flock' (at Micah 4:8) with the locality (Bethlehem) where the Messiah of Israel will inherit the kingdom (see also Targum Pseudo-Jonathan on Gen 35:21). The Palestinian Talmud combines the three elements—Bethlehem, Tower of the Flock,

---

9. House, *Old Testament Theology*, 370. See also Psalm 90:2.

10. John was also aware of this tradition amongst the Jerusalem elite (John 7:42).

Messianic king—in declaring that the Messiah would arise from 'the royal city of Bethlehem of Judah' (*Berakhot* 5a).[11]

Micah concludes his book with a vision of eventual salvation, of the world put right. The final few verses of the book bring together many of the major threads we have been pursuing. Micah 7:14 draws attention to the eschatological shepherd, with the key words "shepherd," "staff," "flock," and "garden"; 7:15 imagines a new Exodus, that great paradigm of final salvation; 7:16 prophesies an international kingdom, extending to "the nations"; 7:17 is a revisiting of the cursing of the snake, with the snake defeated and licking the dust; 7:18 includes a skilful signature of Micah's own name ("who is like Jah?"); and the final verse of the book, verse 20, employs several big covenant words, including *khesed*:

> You will show faithfulness to Jacob and steadfast love to Abraham,
> as you have sworn to our fathers from the days of old. Micah 7:20

God's promise of a Seed to Abraham and to Jacob, and his solemn vows to the tribe of Judah and in particular to David, will be brought to pass. Even, as in Micah's day, when the religious centre is corrupted by wealth and power, God's promise still stands. Hope is alive in unexpected places. Babylon may drag the Jerusalem elite into exile, but under the surface, the Seed is still growing in secret. It may take another seven hundred years, centuries of difficulty and dislocation and silence, but the world will have her Shepherd. Labour pain will give place to peace. The Shepherd, with staff in hand, will rule the nations forever.

11. Vermes, *The Nativity*, 88.

16

Isaiah
The Child and the Snake

The nursing child shall play over the hole of the cobra, and the weaned child shall put his hand on the adder's den.

—Isaiah 11:8

Micah's contemporary Isaiah also delivers a stunning messianic prophecy. Isaiah, like Micah, perceives that although David's great family tree will be cut down, with only its stump remaining, a small shoot will yet come forth from the root of Jesse. Power, influence and riches accrued over generations may all be gone, but the enduring, ancient stump of Jesse still has roots which are alive underground. The dynastic DNA of David, the birth in Bethlehem, is still awaited.

The church may forfeit her Jerusalems, but she will never lose her Bethlehems. She may, for a season, be deprived of her cultural power, her public institutions, her interface with the State, but she will never lose her potential for re-birth. Even in the depths of winter, the bulbs of spring lie dormant beneath the surface, packed full of potential energy.

Isaiah 11:1–10 is one poem, topped and tailed by references to the stump of Jesse. The first half of the poem (verses 1–5) describes the ideal, awaited king. The second half (verses 6–10) describes the Edenic new creation that he will inaugurate. The ideal king sounds a lot like David, arising from Jesse, with the seven-fold Spirit resting upon him, and discernment rather than "what his eyes see," which harks back to "man looks on the outward appearance, but God looks on the heart" (1 Sam 16:7). In the idyllic Eden resulting from his reign, we see this king as a new Adam, antagonistic animals finding peace together, and the whole land enjoying rest. No fear. No war. What a king! Palestinian theologian Yohanna Katanacho demonstrates that in Scripture there is always a relationship between the godliness of the rulers and the state of the land,

> The meaning and nature of the land are strongly associated with the nature of its masters. Whenever injustice dominates, the land suffers and its inhabitants are not at peace; but whenever its inhabitants are godly, it flourishes and overflows with blessings. Further, when Isaiah describes the land in a state of rest, he uses images of new creation where peace and security prevail (Isaiah 11).[1]

And in verse 8, Isaiah casts a vision about a Child who is not afraid of snakes. Ever since Eden we have been waiting for a serpent-slayer. We knew he would be the Seed of the woman. What we never fully realised, not until Isaiah, was that the snake-trampling, Spirit-anointed, new-creation-inaugurating king would be a Child. How can the Child play by the hole of the snake? Because the snake is gone. How can a Child put his hand into the adder's den? Because the adder has been rendered venom-less. Nothing impure may enter this new Eden—the snake is unclean. Nothing dangerous may threaten this regained paradise—the snake is banished. Where Adam failed, the Child succeeds.

This is not the first time Isaiah, in his visions, has seen the Child. In recent chapters, the Child has been repeatedly entering Isaiah's consciousness. Firstly, the Child will be virgin-born:

> Therefore the Lord himself will give you a sign. Behold, the virgin shall conceive and bear a son, and shall call his name Immanuel. Isaiah 7:14

---

1. Katanacho, *The Land of Christ: A Palestinian Cry,* 32.

Then again, in the most famous of Christmas readings, a child-gift is prophesied.

> For to us a child is born,
> to us a son is given;
> and the government shall be upon his shoulder,
> and his name shall be called
> Wonderful Counsellor, Mighty God,
> Everlasting Father, Prince of Peace.
> Of the increase of his government and of peace
> there will be no end,
> on the throne of David and over his kingdom,
> to establish it and to uphold it
> with justice and with righteousness
> from this time forth and forevermore.
> The zeal of the LORD of hosts will do this. Isaiah 9:6–7

Isaiah 9 carries the new creation theme of light shining in darkness, reminiscent of Genesis 1. The Child-king will sit on David's throne. He will bring peace.

Later in Isaiah, the prophet will speak of labour and birth in several places (Is 26:16–18, 54:1). For example,

> Before she was in labour she gave birth; before her pain came upon
> her she delivered a son. Isaiah 66:7

For the prophet Isaiah, it is clear and pertinent that Messiah will somehow be a Child.

CHILD AS RESISTANCE

The main power of the Child motif is a portrayal of innocence. In the face of uncleanness, the triumph of purity. In the face of tyranny, non-violent resistance. The weak shame the strong, and the unarmed and defenceless shame the weaponised. This is Bethlehem. We saw childlikeness in the early David viz-a-viz Saul, and we see it in baby Jesus, sent unarmed and defenceless into a violent world. We saw it in Pharaoh versus the babies (Ex 1:22), and we will see it again in Herod versus the babies (Matt 2:16), both evil kings sending kill-teams to slaughter innocent Jewish children. In the abhorrent history of our genocidal world, soldiers killing babies has been far too common.

There is something in the power of this contrast that puts the armed occupier to shame. Many of the stencilled graffiti pictures on the Bethlehem side of the wall also carry this theme of childlike innocence. A happy toddler skipping, but her skipping rope is barbed wire. A young child on its knees, seemingly praying. A young boy with what looks like a toy diabolo, or Chinese yo-yo, but instead of strings he is holding barbed wire, and instead of a wooden diabolo, he is juggling a rocket shell. A soldier, in full combat gear with a rifle in his hand, swinging a barbed wire skipping rope for a young girl. A foetus wrapped up in a barbed wire womb. These images are grainy, visceral, mostly black stencils on grey concrete, and the point they make is stark. Cakes Stencils, who is one of the prominent resistance artists in the community growing around Banksy's Walled Off Hotel installation, employs images of children in his art in order to signify a loss of innocence. "Kids don't understand things like race or nationhood. It's a distinction made by those in power . . . adults."[2]

Within the lobby of the Walled Off Hotel, Banksy's most emotive piece takes pride of place. A Palestinian child holding a toy mallet sits by the concrete wall, out of which has been crudely carved an enormous heart, a window through to the other side. "Only innocence and love can dismantle this wall," the picture seems to say. The first time I laid eyes on this piece, I sobbed and sobbed in front of it. The defencelessness of children exacerbates the brutality of the soldiers, the inhumanity of concrete and iron, the unnaturalness of war. It is the ultimate image for resistance art.

CHILD AS RETURN TO INNOCENCE

The other compelling feeling evoked by Isaiah's Child is a yearning for innocence, a longing for a simpler, purer time. The stump of Jesse, according to 11:3, will "smell" the fear of the Lord, attuned to God and far from the corruption and lack of discernment of normal rulers. In the return to Eden, the Child will lead the parading animals, and antagonistic animals will lay down together (11:6). The disharmony between man and his environment will be removed. Padilla DeBorst's phrase for this is a "just conviviality,"[3] a re-balancing of relationships, human and ecological, according to the principles of divine justice. Chapter 11 goes on to speak of Jews and Gentiles being brought together by the Child-king. For commentator Beale,

2. Holdsworth, "Cakes Stencils."

3. Padilla DeBorst, "Community and Just Conviviality."

the harmonious relationship of previously antagonistic animals is a picture of end-time fellowship that will occur between Jew and Gentile. "There should be no divisions of people groups in the new creation, just as there was to be no such division in the first creation."[4] The lack of antagonism among animals and the lack of division among humanity is a recapitulation of the original paradisical conditions of Eden.[5] Biblical scholar Beale and resistance artist Cakes Stencils are saying the same thing—children are the key to reconciliation.

This theme is consistent with Micah's evocation of Bethlehem as a place of non-corrupt new beginnings, over against the sophisticated corruption of Jerusalem. Where Micah draws the distinction as urban-pastoral, Isaiah draws it as adult-child. The same yearning is being tapped into—a basic human nostalgia for a simpler time.

JESUS, THE CHILD OF BETHLEHEM

Thus, Isaiah's innovation in the unfolding Bethlehem story is to note that the awaited Messiah will be a Child. Jesus, born in Bethlehem, at a time when Jesse's tree was all but gone, born naked and vulnerable, pursued by Herod's soldiers, born under Roman occupation, will lead God's people in reconciliation, in peace-making, in a return to innocence.

The subversive, disarming power of meekness is seen repeatedly in the ministry of Jesus. In the sermon on the mount, to a people under brutal Roman occupation, Jesus' teaching about turning the other cheek demonstrates this principle of non-violent resistance. Katanacho, speaking as a Palestinian under Israeli occupation, explains that a slap on the right cheek is a "dehumanising, discriminatory, humiliating action." In offering the other cheek, something happens in the wronged party, who is changed in that moment "from a victim to a missionary." Injustice is exposed for what it truly is, is shown to be shameful.[6] According to Munther Isaac:

> [Jesus] embodied the prophetic tradition, humbly and gently challenging the power structures by introducing a new kingdom that embodies and elevates the realities of justice over power, equality

4. Beale, *A New Testament Biblical Theology*, 876.
5. Beale, *A New Testament Biblical Theology*, 877.
6. Katanacho, "Palestininan Orthopathos."

over superiority, humility over pride, peace over violence, and love over bigotry.[7]

When the disciples, jostling for honour, ask Jesus "Who is the greatest in the kingdom of heaven?" he replies by placing a young child in the centre of the group. Jesus, the greatest resistance artist from Bethlehem, is painting a picture not unlike those of Cakes Stencils or Banksy. The simplicity of the child is contrasted with the ambition and rivalry of the disciples. Jesus puts them to shame, calls them to repent, calls them to abase themselves.[8]

In the Parable of the Wicked Tenants, Jesus, a few days before his crucifixion, expounds a profound principle in God's sending of a child to kill the snake. God's soliloquy is related by Luke:

> Then the owner of the vineyard said, "What shall I do? I will send my beloved son; perhaps they will respect him." Luke 20:13

Bailey draws out the powerful language of honour and shame in this parable, explaining that the non-violence of the son ought to shame the tenants into repentance.

> Most Arabic versions of the last thousand years have translated this key phrase literally with *yastahiyun minhu* (they will feel shame in his presence). Retaliation is not the only way. The costly path of total vulnerability has the power to be life-renewing. . . . The violent option would only trigger further violence.[9]

God sends his son, an unarmed and defenceless child, into a world in full-blown rebellion—this is the power of the incarnation. This is the message of Bethlehem. All over the world, Christians finding themselves in situations of oppression, discrimination and disempowerment are urged to lean into Christ's example, the power of childlike meekness, in order to cast shame on their oppressors. The Kairos Document, written by an ecumenical group of Palestinian Christian leaders, calls for this non-violent, creative resistance:

> We say that our option as Christians in the face of the Israeli occupation is to resist. Resistance is a right and a duty for the Christian. But it is resistance with love as its logic. It is thus a creative

---

7. Isaac, *The Other Side*, 66.

8. *Tapeinoo*; to bring low, depress, level, to humble, abase. Mounce, *Analytical Lexicon*, 444.

9. Bailey, *Middle Eastern Eyes*, 419.

resistance for it must find human ways that engage the humanity of the enemy. Seeing the image of God in the face of the enemy means taking up positions in the light of this vision of active resistance to stop the injustice and oblige the perpetrator to end his aggression and thus achieve the desired goal, which is getting back the land, freedom, dignity and independence.[10]

The example of Jesus, in his birth, his life, his teaching and his death, declares that childlike meekness will in the end be vindicated. Finally, in Revelation 12, where all the threads of the Bethlehem story eventually coalesce, it is the Child who slays the dragon. Isaiah's vision is fulfilled in Jesus, the Unafraid, the Unarmed, the Innocent, Jesus who disarms and humiliates rulers and authorities (Col 2:15) through his own disarmament and humiliation in incarnation and crucifixion. The power of powerlessness, the might of meekness, the beauty of Bethlehem, must never be underestimated.

10. Katanacho, *The Land of Christ: A Palestinian Cry,* 84.

17

Jeremiah
Rachel Weeping

Thus says the LORD: "A voice is heard in Ramah, lamentation and bitter weeping. Rachel is weeping for her children; she refuses to be comforted for her children, because they are no more."

—JEREMIAH 31:15

AT ISRAEL'S DARKEST HOUR, in the concentration camp at Ramah on the eve of their long march into exile (Jer 40:1), rag-tag Israel gathers around the aging Jeremiah as he pours forth prophecy dripping with hope. He prophesies a re-gathering of the scattered, mourning turned to joy, replenishing for every languishing soul. He prophesies a new covenant, new hearts, a new spirit. Jeremiah 31 is majestic, soaring poetry. And yet, right in the middle of this hope-filled, joyful declaration about the future, interjects verse 15. The haunting sound of Rachel weeping for her children.

Ramah, most famously the home village of the prophet Samuel, was a stopping-place on the road heading north from Jerusalem. It lay, nestled among the olive groves, in the territory of Benjamin, close to Gibeah of Saul (Judg 19:13) and not too far from Jeremiah's hometown of Anathoth. Here, the Babylonian commander Nebuzaradan gathered up all the residents of Jerusalem and Judea who were to be marched thousands of miles into exile. Ragged, broken, silent, the sheep of Israel with their few meagre belongings congregated at Ramah in preparation for the long trek. They knew they would never see home again. They knew it was all over. They huddled down into their blankets and waited for the order to march.

> Thus, in the fateful year 586 B.C. Jerusalem fell. It was the end of the house of David as a temporal dynasty, the end of Judah as a sovereign state, the end of Jerusalem as a fortress. But it was the beginning, as Jeremiah already dimly perceived, of a new Jerusalem made without hands, of the House of David spiritually supreme amongst the kings of the earth, and of a conquered People conquering the world by suffering and faith.[1]

Ramah would live long in the collective Jewish memory as a weighty, emotionally-fraught place name, much as Auschwitz would 2,500 years later.

The Benjamites also venerated Ramah as the place where Rachel was buried (1 Sam 10:2). Rachel's tomb is near Bethlehem, but the people of Benjamin would have wanted a tradition venerating Rachel (she is *their* mother, after all) within their own territory rather than under the jurisdiction of their arch-rival, Judah. This would not be the last time tombs of saints were claimed in rival locations. Historians have struggled with this incongruity—surely Rachel can only be buried in one place? It does seem that Rachel is genuinely part of the Bethlehem story, and she rests at the bottom of the hill, close to Checkpoint 300. However Jeremiah (who grew up in Anathoth in Benjamin), is referring to his local tradition that Rachel is present and weeping over the exiles in Ramah.

Between verses 14 and 15 there is a crunching gear change. Jeremiah has been prophesying future return—beyond imagining in the circumstances—a future full of dancing and feasting and joy. Then, in verse 15, the prophet switches to a minor key, moves into a mode of lament, and in so doing, immortalises Rachel. He imagines that mother in Israel, the one who herself was buried "on the way," who never arrived but was frozen in a perpetual state of non-belonging, weeping bitter tears for her children. Rachel, who understood shame, who epitomised grief, whose sons were exiled to Egypt, is pictured praying for her descendants as they once again take to the road.

1. Caiger, *Lives of the Prophets*, 216.

There is a nod to Hannah in the text. Hannah, who was from Ramah, "was deeply distressed and prayed to the Lord and wept bitterly" (1 Sam 1:10) Rachel is imagined by Jeremiah to be weeping bitterly in prayer. And, as Hannah's prayer is heard and she conceives a son, she names him Samuel, meaning "God hears." In the same way, in Jeremiah's prophecy, God hears Rachel's prayer.

> Thus says the LORD: "Keep your voice from weeping, and your eyes from tears, for there is a reward for your work, declares the LORD, and they shall come back from the land of the enemy. There is hope for your future, declares the LORD, and your children shall come back to their own country. Jeremiah 31:16–17

Because of these verses, later Jewish tradition came to think of Rachel as a great intercessor. Rabbi Shimon ben Yohai claimed that "everything depended upon Rachel."[2] Rachel's tears draw an answer from God, they are counted as prayer. In another tradition, both Abraham and Moses pray for Israel after the destruction of the Jerusalem temple, but it is only when Rachel intercedes that God responds (Lamentations Rabbah 24).[3]

When Matthew quotes Jeremiah 31:15 in the context of Herod's slaughter of the innocents, he is drawing a line from Genesis 35, through Jeremiah 31, to the birth of Jesus Christ. Lament is part of new beginnings. Only through something dying does something new come to birth. Even in the midst of incredible joy, the presence of bitter tears is not to be denied. The shock and grief and anger of the mothers of Bethlehem falls as tears which water the Christ-seed, and hope begins to germinate. Exile was part of Rachel's story, part of Israel's story, and part of Christ's story too. Bitter tears over refugees, over mindless slaughter, over the disinherited, are biblical. Strickert draws our focus onto the liminal nature of grief, embodied by Rachel's tears, noting that Jews and Christians read Jeremiah 31 at their respective New Year festivals, Jews in September and Christians in December.

> For nearly two millennia Jews and Christians have reminded themselves of the on-the-way character of the life of faith, reading these words of Rachel weeping at the transition point of human life, the New Year. For Christians this takes place at the commemoration of the Slaughter of the Innocents on December 28 at the end of the calendar year. For Jews, the reading occurs at the

2. *Gen. Rabbah* 71:2.

3. Pitre, *Jewish Roots of Mary,* 168.

beginning, on Rosh Hashanah II. People of all faiths can resonate with Rachel because they, too, are people of faith.[4]

When Matthew cites this verse in 2:18, he sees Rachel's tears as prophetic of return and restoration taking place through pain, the Jeremiah context: Though you are exiled and abandoned, I will bring you back! Rachel, watching from her Bethlehem vantage-point, weeps as Herod's kill teams deploy up the hill to slaughter all the boys under two years of age, a paranoid Usurper desperately trying to hold onto his throne as the rightful is born. This horrific event never made it into any extra-biblical historical sources, causing some to question its veracity, but most massacres of the defenceless in the margins of the world never make the news. Besides, the number of children, relatively speaking, was not large. Brown does the maths: "Because of the high infant mortality rate, we are told that if the total population was one thousand, with an annual birth-rate of thirty, the male children under two years of age would scarcely have numbered more than twenty."[5]

Twenty, but mostly extended family of Jesus. His cousins, second cousins, his kin. Twenty, and unnoticed by the world, but grieved in Scripture and remembered by the church. Tears flowing again in Bethlehem. Herod, almost seventy, increasingly paranoid, violent, evil, wracked with pain and vengeful bloodlust in his final years, drives Joseph and Mary into exile, fleeing for their lives. Jesus Christ was a refugee. At the centre of our faith is a vulnerable, stateless person. A God on the wrong side of history. The Archbishop of Canterbury, Justin Welby, put it like this in the Foreword to Krish Kandiah's book *God is Stranger*:

> The 'God of Abraham, Isaac and Jacob' is a God of wanderers, of aliens and refugees. The God of the displaced. The God of those who just do not belong. The God whose people, and presence, is in 'all the wrong places', to use Kandiah's phrase. All too often, when we ask, 'Where is God?' it is because we want a God of power: a God who will come and sort the world out, overriding human selfishness and injustice, putting things right from above. Instead, we discover a God who chooses to come quietly and dwell with the poor and the oppressed, the refugee and the alien.[6]

4. Strickert, *Rachel Weeping*, xvi.

5. Brown, *Birth of the Messiah*, 204.

6. Welby, "Foreword," Kindle Location 78.

This presence of God with a people pursued and persecuted is central to the Jewish story. The presence of God in Christ the refugee is central to the Bethlehem story. No wonder Rachel is weeping, and refusing to be comforted.

THE IMPORTANCE OF LAMENT

Lament is the beginning of prophecy, grief is protest. Jeremiah, often called the weeping prophet, knows the importance of lamentation. Grief, lament, tears, are an important genre in the Bible, an essential idiom for the prophet. Where the tone of empire is frequently one of optimism and satiation, the tone of the margins is more often one of hunger and dislocation, a visceral cry that things are not right. Brueggemann's view is that prophetic, poetic lament interrupts the narcoticised, unfeeling narratives of the centre, which are necessarily in prose. Verse interrupts prose. Grief breaks silence. Silence, that successful strategy for maintaining the status quo, is shattered by the cry of an anguished heart.

> Every totalitarian regime is frightened of the artist. It is the vocation of the prophet to keep alive the ministry of imagination, to keep on conjuring and proposing futures alternative to the single one the king wants to urge as the only thinkable one. Indeed, poetic imagination is the last way left in which to challenge and conflict the dominant reality.[7]

Part of Jeremiah's role, as a prophet, was to disrupt the dominant narrative. With the Jerusalem elite saying "peace, peace," in an attempt to keep the status quo functioning, Jeremiah was a disruptive, unpopular, unpalatable, inconvenient voice from the margins, weeping passionate tears and baring his bitter soul.[8] "Real criticism," writes Brueggemann, "begins in the capacity to grieve, because that is the most visceral announcement that things are not right."[9]

Alison Phipps, in a completely different world from Brueggemann, the world not of biblical studies but of postcolonial studies, also recognises the value of the artist in challenging accepted views of the world.

---

7. Brueggemann, *Prophetic Imagination*, Kindle Location 1151.
8. Jeremiah 8:11, and other places.
9. Brueggemann, *Prophetic Imagination*, Kindle Location 625.

> If we are going to do this, we will need artists and poetic activists
> to break the hold of the discourse of the colonising . . . speaking
> words which change the dull echo-chambers of the soundscape;
> speaking words which are not a backing track but which will be
> heard. . . . And poetry remains, according to the Welsh poet writ-
> ing from within what he understood as colonial conditions, "that
> which enters the intellect, by way of the heart." (R. S. Thomas)"[10]

Poetic activism is exactly what most of the Hebrew prophets were pursuing, employing verse, sarcasm, surprise, sometimes mischief and humour, often grief, anything to jar, to confound, to grab the attention. Where the histories, the Samuels and Kings and Chronicles of this world, are written in prose, their prophetic critiques are coined in verse. In this way, marginal prophets are not only saying, "your flat imperial narrative of prosperity and progress doesn't extend to me, doesn't stretch from Rome or Jerusalem as far as Bethlehem, we are excluded from your story," they are going beyond that to criticism, "your narrative is inadequate, your supposed objectivity not objective, your policies unjust, your presumption of divine sanction misplaced." This is poetry as protest.

So lament is a powerful prophetic idiom for the rupturing of the mainstream, dispassionate story of safety and security. Grief, which is so subjective, so personal, penetrates and disrupts the scientific, objective hermeneutics of the centre. That which is merely collateral damage, which wouldn't have made the news cycle in the volatile borderlands of the Babylonian empire, is registered as bitter tears in a specific place, Ramah, from a specific mother, Rachel. The deaths of a few baby boys in a tiny village, a small price to pay for the greater good of Jerusalem's security and prosperity under Herod, even if it never made the history books, is now commemorated in the Christian tradition by millions worldwide annually. Yes, Bethlehem is a place of tears, and they are tears of protest, grief as resistance, lament as prophecy.

With so many of the messianic oracles about Bethlehem being in verse, not prose, we find the Bethlehem story is amongst the prophets. Like these lines from Jeremiah 31, this longing is part of the prophetic hope-fuelled resistance against the status quo. Jesse's root will come and change everything. When the Seed comes, he will reboot the world. We need the discontinuity of new creation because the old creation is corrupt beyond repair. Jesus, when he came, came full of feeling. "Blessed are those who

10. Phipps, *Decolonising Multilingualism*, 9.

mourn," he said, and then God stood at the tomb of his friend Lazarus and he wept.

CRYING STARTS WITH SEEING

Privilege can blind. Not always. Not exclusively. But often. Ezekiel's commentary on the sin of Sodom as "pride, excess of food and prosperous ease" (16:49), is issued as a warning to Jerusalem. Sometimes, the full just don't notice the hungry, and the role of the prophet is to help them to see. Boaz is an example of someone with resources whose eyes were open, who noticed Ruth. Flemming Rutledge puts it in this way, "The beginning of resistance is not to explain, but to see."[11] When we notice, we feel. When we feel, we weep. When we weep, we pray. When we pray, we act.

Prophetic lament, like Rachel's tears here in Jeremiah 31, ruptures the complacency of privilege and opens eyes to the pain and dislocation in the margins of our world. Boazes notice Ruths, and welcome them into the House of Bread. Grief, that inconvenient, jarring cry, breaks the silence of the status quo, puts change on the agenda, calls for justice. Bethlehem's story has uncomfortable moments. The Christmas story has unsettling aspects. This is important. Rachel's bitter tears are part of the human experience. The Ramahs of this world should never be forgotten. The East is good at remembering, the West less so. Our propensity as humans to destroy one another is part of the apologetic for Messiah. Our complicity, our victimhood, our shame, our need of a Saviour.

Let us weep.

11. Rutledge, *The Crucifixion,* 434.

18

Joseph
Shame-Removal

And her husband Joseph, being a just man and unwilling to put her to shame, resolved to divorce her quietly. But as he considered these things, behold, an angel of the Lord appeared to him in a dream, saying, "Joseph, son of David, do not fear to take Mary as your wife, for that which is conceived in her is from the Holy Spirit."

—MATTHEW 1:19–20

MARY'S LIFE WAS IN danger. To people in the Middle East, this is obvious. The presence of a pregnant, unmarried woman threatens the honour of the whole village. Matthews writes that, "if a household could not protect its women, then it was declared insolvent or shamed and unable to fulfil its responsibilities to the community as a whole."[1] The ability of the men of the community to protect the chastity of their women is a basic indicator of "honourableness," and the Nazareth community would be in a major spin as soon as the gossip started flowing. "Honour killings" are a common

1. Matthews, "Honor and Shame," 104.

response in such situations, even today in some places. Whether or not Mary was guilty had nothing to do with it. Even if one of Herod's soldiers had forced himself on her, the shame was just as real. Community honour, in this sense, is like balance. Mary's dishonour would bring imbalance to her father's house, her extended family, and to the reputation of the whole village. Action must be taken to remove the shame and restore balance.[2]

"The family will kill her!" declares Mansour, who is a shepherd in modern-day Bethlehem, matter-of-factly, in a series of video interviews with Bethlehemites about the Christmas story. Aisha, who is a local midwife, explains, "The honour killing. In our land, she must be married. It's shame for us." *For us* her means for the whole community—the shame stains all of us. Rana, interviewed alongside Aisha, adds another option. "If she's not killed, she will be thrown from her home."[3] These are normal responses across the region to an unmarried pregnancy. Two thousand years ago, Mary's position was, if anything, even more vulnerable. When Luke records Mary's response to the angel, "Let it be to me according to your word" (1:38), her courage in the face of probable death or ostracism is on display. In the very next verse, we read that Mary "arose and went with haste" down to the hill country of Judah to visit Elizabeth (v. 39). The haste implies that she wanted to get away quickly. She stayed with Zechariah and Elizabeth three months, and then returned home to Nazareth (v. 56). Three months pregnant, and starting to show.

While Luke's narrative focuses on Mary (with enough detail to suggest that Luke had the opportunity to interview Mary in detail as part of the research for his book), Matthew's telling focuses on Joseph. How did Joseph feel, and what were his options, when his fiancée, "before they came together [sexually] . . . was found to be with child" (Matt 1:18)? Joseph, essentially, had three options available to him. We will call these justice, mercy and grace.

Justice would have involved Joseph acting in line with conservative community expectations and Deuteronomy 22:21. He would have accused Mary publicly of adultery. As her fiancé and accuser, Joseph would have cast the first stone. This would happen at the door of her father's house, to shame the family who could not protect their daughter's chastity. Then, following his example, the whole community would have picked up stones

2. E.g. Sedanur Guzel, a nine-year-old girl who was raped and then killed by stoning in Kars, Turkey, 2018.

3. St Paul's Auckland, "O Little Town of Bethlehem."

to throw until she lay dead. The whole community, summoning their deep revulsion to shame and their determination to keep its contagion away from their homes and their children, to clear the name of their village, to show that they tolerate no exceptions. Stoning is significant. The entire community has been insulted, and so the entire community must correct the balance. Death by stoning allows the whole village to be involved.

There is clear evidence that, in ancient Israel, girls were usually betrothed to a man at age 12 or 13, and then taken into their husband's home around one year later. This contract of engagement was a public and binding agreement between two families, and entirely predicated on the virginity of the bride. In Galilee, according to the Rabbis, this in-between year was very strictly enforced, to make sure that no opportunity for any accusation could arise.

Frymer-Kensky puts some colour on this state of affairs:

> If something bad happens to her, it not only causes her kin sorrow and loss, it also reflects poorly on the patriarch's ability to protect his family. If she does something of which her family or society might not approve, it is a sign that the father/husband cannot control his relatives. The family is dishonored and loses political and economic influence. The honor of the family and its ability to marry off its children advantageously depend on the honor of the father.[4]

The virginity of a man's daughters is the basic currency of village life. If a man cannot protect the honour of his women, he will be shunned. No-one will do business with him, no-one will give or receive in marriage. That's why the bride's family would ensure they got wedding night evidence of the girl's virginity—blood-stained sheets to show that her maidenhead was intact (Deuteronomy 22:17) as a piece of physical, public evidence of their success.

Even a cursory look at novels, soap operas or films set in the modern Middle East show that this whole subject is still of major concern today. Egyptian novelist el Saadawi describes a virginity test on a wedding night: the men's honour depends upon the bride's intact hymen.

> Blood poured out onto the white towel which was held high to flutter above people's heads. The women let out a chorus of shrill *you yous* and the drums beat. The breasts of the men and the hus-bands could now swell and their noses rise as high as the ceiling

4. Frymer-Kensky, *Women of the Bible*, 180.

above. For honour meant the honour of the male, even if the proof of it was in the body of the female.[5]

Mary being found pregnant is a failure of her father and an insult to her fiancé. Joseph, keen to obey the law and defend his own family reputation, should by rights accuse Mary, cast the first stone, and purge every hint of uncleanness away through the shedding of blood: justice.

But Joseph could not kill Mary. Matthew tells us clearly that Joseph, without dwelling on option one, had moved straight to option two: *mercy*.

> And her husband Joseph, being a just man and unwilling to put her to shame, resolved to divorce her quietly. Matthew 1:19

Joseph is unwilling to expose Mary to public punishment. He is unwilling to accuse her before the village. Maybe because he loves her. Maybe because he can't stomach seeing a thirteen-year-old girl lynched. His plan is to "divorce her quietly." He resolves to speak to Mary's father and break off the engagement. He will distance himself from the shame. Mary will continue to live in her father's house, she will give birth to an illegitimate child, the village will gossip and ostracise and stop dealing with that family. At least she won't be dead, but her life will not really be a life. She is unlikely to marry. She will live, friendless and alone, a virtual prisoner in her father's house, for the rest of her days. This is what Joseph was considering—mercy. Better than a direct accusation and execution, but Mary would live under a cloud of suspicion, with pariah-status, for the rest of her life.

> But as he considered these things, behold, an angel of the Lord appeared to him in a dream, saying, "Joseph, son of David, do not fear to take Mary as your wife, for that which is conceived in her is from the Holy Spirit. She will bear a son, and you shall call his name Jesus, for he will save his people from their sins." Matthew 1:20–21

"But as he considered these things" includes the Greek word *enthymeomai*. "Considered" is a very English under-translation. The root word, *thymos*, means "wrath" or "anger." Joseph, as he thought about Mary's pregnancy and his options, felt a deep anger burning inside. He was fuming (Prov 6:34–35)! The *Protoevangelium of James*[6] 14:1 shows something of his

---

5. el Saadawi, *The Innocence of the Devil*, 43.
6. A second century extra-Biblical book about the birth of Jesus.

deep moral dilemma: "If I hide her sin, I am fighting the Law of the Lord." Bailey's study of Matthew 1:20 helps us to understand this word.

> Perhaps long centuries of veneration for "Saint Joseph," have led to an assumption that he could not have become angry—particularly not with Mary! But this is to overlook the pure humanness of the man. On hearing that his fiancée was pregnant, is he expected to sit quietly and "consider" this matter? Or would he naturally feel deeply disappointed and indeed angry? As observed, his under-standing of justice led him to "do the right thing" and treat Mary in a humane fashion. But did that prevent him from feeling the anger of betrayal?[7]

As Joseph is fuming over this impossible situation, an angel appears in his dream and addresses him as "Joseph, son of David" (v. 20). The angel is saying, "Remember your ancestors. Remember Salmon and Boaz, who nobly absorbed shame through marriage. Remember Judah who was qualified for leadership by laying down his life. Remember David who covered Mephibosheth's lameness. You come from a long line of courageous venom-absorbers, shame-removers and grace-displayers. Don't be afraid to take Mary into your home;" a phrase meaning step two of the betrothal process, taking Mary as his legal wife.

The angel also tells Joseph to name the baby. To name a child is to assume legal paternity for them. By taking Mary and the unborn child into his home, Joseph is assuming public responsibility for them. By naming the child ("You shall call his name Jesus" (v. 21)), Joseph is acknowledging him as his own. Catholic scholar Raymond Brown, in his unrivalled study of the infancy narratives, explains "legal paternity" in this way:

> The Jewish position on this is lucidly clear and is dictated by the fact that sometimes it is difficult to determine who begot a child biologically. Since normally a man will not acknowledge and sup-port a child unless it is his own, the law prefers to base paternity on the man's acknowledgement. The Mishna *baba Bathra* 8:6 states the principle: "If a man says, 'This is my son,' he is to be believed." Joseph, by exercising the father's right to name the child, acknowl-edges Jesus and thus becomes the legal father of the child[8].

It can be hard in the West to understand "legal paternity," but many ancient societies preserved this distinction. In Sparta, biological fatherhood

---

7. Bailey, *Middle Eastern Eyes*, 45.

8. Brown, *Birth of the Messiah*, 139.

was immaterial and only sociological fatherhood (who raised the child) counted. In Rome, there was a distinction between the *progenitor* and the *pater*.[9] Joseph's naming of Jesus would have diffused the community's outrage.

This third option, the divinely-infused, angelically-inspired, game-changing action of Joseph, we can call *grace*. Joseph bravely declares the child his own. All the judgement and suspicion shifts away from Mary and towards him. His life is not in danger, but his reputation is tarnished. He suffers an honour-decrease in the community that will dog him the rest of his life. As a venom-absorber, though, he turns the poison of the community's resentment away from Mary and towards himself. He takes the blame. He shoulders, in the tradition of Judah, responsibility for the vulnerable Other. He shows, as a Bethlehemite, hospitality towards Mary, and towards the baby she is carrying, acceptance not rejection, at great personal cost. Grace is self-sacrificial. It moves towards shame, at cost to self, and removes it through absorption. Mary gained by association with Joseph. Joseph lost by association with Mary. An exchange took place, with Mary the beneficiary.

> In his cameo appearance, Matthew presents Joseph as a human being of remarkable spiritual stature. He possessed the boldness, daring, courage and strength of character to stand up against his entire community and take Mary as his wife. He did so in spite of forces that no doubt wanted her stoned. His vision of justice stayed his hand. In short, he was able to reprocess his anger into grace.[10]

Gossip and accusations surrounding his birth would dog Jesus his whole life. For example, in John 8:41 his opponents imply that he was illegitimate, in an attempt to discredit him. There is another sly accusation of illegitimacy in Mark 6:3.[11] But Joseph's marriage of Mary and naming of the child are enough to legally secure Jesus a place in the world, in the line of David, and in the immediate community of Nazareth in Galilee.

Later, Jesus will show similar empathy for the falsely-accused, and for women whose lot was unfair in a strongly patriarchal society. When a woman caught in adultery is about to suffer stoning, Jesus interposes himself between the accusers and the victim, boldly challenges the crowd,

9. Frymer-Kensky, "Virginity in the Bible," 85.

10. Bailey, *Middle Eastern Eyes*, 46.

11. For ongoing claims of Jesus' illegitimacy by opponents of Christianity, see *Acts of Pilate* 2:3, *Against Celsus* 1:28, 32, *De Spectaculis* 30:6.

"let him who is without sin among you be the first to throw a stone at her" (John 8:7), and neatly turns the anger of the mob away from the woman and onto himself. By the end of the chapter, it is not the woman, but Jesus whom they are seeking to stone (v. 59). No doubt, he was thinking of his mother and following the example of his step-father.

Joseph was a prophet, and he shows us something about God. The same three choices that Joseph had when confronted with Mary's shame are, in a cosmic sense, the options before the Divine when confronted with the shame and spiritual adultery of mankind (the difference being that Mary was innocent, whereas mankind is guilty as charged). Option one, justice, declares that "the wages of sin is death." God could accuse mankind, cast the first stone, wipe us away and start again. Option two, mercy, would involve God distancing himself from us, leaving us to live on earth in our filth and shame while he lives at arm's length in heaven in his unimpeachable honour. Yet God, at Bethlehem, chose option three—grace. He moved towards our shame. The mockery, humiliation and abhorrence of death on the cross signified God's total identification with our plight, and a divine substitution. Our shame, credited to him. His honour, given to us. He takes responsibility. He marries and names. He assumes legal paternity.

"Now the *genesis* of Jesus Christ took place in this way." Matthew speaks in verse 1 and verse 18, albeit in slightly different noun-forms, of the *genesis* of Jesus. He structures his account first with the genealogy, then with the story, reflecting Genesis 1 and 2, where the origins of creation are told, the first being the numerical pattern of creation, the second being the narrative account. Also, in tracing the genealogy of Messiah, he shows that there were good grounds for Joseph, if he knew his family history, to make such an outrageous, godly, courageous choice.

Bethlehem, then, is once again a place where the grace of God meets the shame of humanity. Where an innocent venom-absorber chooses voluntarily to bear shame, where a shame-substitution takes place.

19

Jesus
Under Empire

In those days a decree went out from Caesar Augustus that all the world
should be registered.

This was the first registration when Quirinius was governor of Syria.

And all went to be registered, each to his own town.

And Joseph also went up from Galilee, from the town of Nazareth, to
Judea, to the city of David, which is called Bethlehem, because he was of the
house and lineage of David,

to be registered with Mary, his betrothed, who was with child.

And while they were there, the time came for her to give birth.

—LUKE 2:1–6

UP THE HILL TO Bethlehem come Joseph and Mary. Empire, that faceless
hegemonic force, seems to control everything about the birth story of Jesus
Christ. Joseph and Mary, two individuals amongst the nameless millions of
those in the margins of the Roman empire, are obliged to travel seventy-odd

miles south to register in Joseph's ancestral village. Raheb compares the Christmas story to the modern Palestinian experience.

> A young couple from Nazareth is forced by the occupiers to go and register. Registration is a means to control those occupied, control their movement, and control their income and taxes. And so Joseph and Mary had to come to Bethlehem to get here their magnetic cards. Then we hear from the Magi, who came from the East to visit the child of Bethlehem and to adore him but were stopped at the borders by Herod's security guards and were harassed and interrogated for the simple reason that they told the truth, in that they are going to Bethlehem. . . . Then we hear of massacres of innocent children dying for no reason except that Herod wanted to terrorize Palestine's population and to spread fear. And then we see the young family seeking refuge in Egypt; they became refugees on the way in order to escape Herod's terror.[1]

Any visitor to the West Bank, after spending an afternoon standing in line at the checkpoint out of Bethlehem, as tempers flare in the stifling heat, and the young, highly-strung Israeli soldiers with their fingers on the trigger dominate the Palestinians in the queue, will have their understanding of the Christmas story profoundly affected. Observing the daily humiliations, small and great, experienced by the occupied cannot help but colour one's reading of the nativity story. It becomes easier to understand why the angels told the shepherds not to be afraid, why first century Jews were praying for a Messiah, why crucifixion was so common and the Romans were so hated, how many frustrated insurrectionists like Barabbas tried to take history into their own hands, why the people were confused about what kind of freedom Jesus was promising, and what kind of liberation he was instigating. Feel life under empire, it will help you read the Bible.

In the eyes of modern residents of Bethlehem, the Israeli occupation is illegal and oppressive. Katanacho writes,

> We are created in the image of God and sinning against a human being is actually sinning against God. From this point of view, occupation is a sin because it dehumanizes people whom God created. The separation wall, the numerous checkpoints and land-grabbing policies are some of the examples of such dehumanization. Occupation manifests both personal sins and structural injustice. Indeed, occupation is not only a form of political

---

1. Raheb, "Christmas Eve Sermon."

oppression; it is also an insult to God because it insults human beings who are created in the image of God.[2]

This latest occupation of Palestine is nothing new. A tiny corridor sandwiched between mighty world powers, the Holy Land has almost always been controlled by powerful neighbours and their imperial ambitions. The Egyptians, Assyrians, Babylonians, Persians, Greeks, Romans, Arabs, Crusaders, Ottomans, British and Israelis have all left their mark on this blood-and-tears-drenched land. Palestine the peripheral, the insignificant, somewhere that needed controlling so that armies and trade could march through on their way to somewhere more important.

Just as the physical land of Palestine and her historic residents have known millennia-worth of occupation and oppression, so too the Jewish people, throughout their history both biblical and post-biblical, wherever they have found themselves in the world, have known what it is to be stigmatised, persecuted, ethnically cleansed: by Egypt, by Babylon, by Rome, the Inquisition, the Pogroms, the Nazis. A Nativity Under Empire is consonant both with the story of Palestine as a place, and with the story of the Jews as a people. The suffering of both is unforgotten.

Jesus' birth under empire as part of an oppressed people with limited freedoms demonstrates the identification of the incarnate with the disempowered. Identification becomes a significant mode of mission, God's fleshification among the conquered shows us something profound about God. And yet, overriding the whims of emperors, the consistent sovereign purposes of God prevail—as he had always promised, the Christ is born in Bethlehem.

> The gospel is this: When the fullness of time came, the time for the Word to be incarnated, God did not choose Rome or Athens for Christ to be born at; He chose occupied Bethlehem. He chose to be one of those oppressed; He chose to be one of those terrorized. When the fullness of time came, God so loved this world with all its ugliness and did not shy away from it. God chose to encounter this world with all its might and terror. He chose to challenge Herod with the face of an innocent child.[3]

The incarnation is God's volitional solidarity with those who suffer. The gospel is most at home in the place of tears. The light shines brightest

---

2. Katanacho, *The Land of Christ: A Palestinian Cry*, 53–54.

3. Raheb, "Christmas Eve Sermon."

in the darkness. The babe is born amongst the broken. Jesus does not come to the centre of the empire (Rome), or to the major administrative city of his province (Caesarea), or even to his people's spiritual capital (Jerusalem). Jesus was born in Bethlehem, at a time when Palestine was occupied by Rome. Right on the margins. In a tiny village in an insignificant territory in a forgotten corner of the empire.

INCARNATION AS SOLIDARITY

Ateek speaks of the significance of Christ's solidarity with the occupied:

> Jesus is the powerless Palestinian humiliated at a checkpoint, the woman trying to get through to the hospital for treatment, the young man whose dignity is trampled, the young student who cannot get to the university to study, the unemployed father who needs to find bread to feed his family.[4]

For those under empire, anywhere in the world, the truth of the incarnation is of enormous comfort. That God chooses to be present in Christ within our suffering, that God is proximate and empathetic—these are wonderful truths. So often the dominant power appeals to God-language to validate their agenda, from Solomon and his heirs, through Herod's temple project, the Crusades, the Inquisition, to more modern colonialisms. When Jerusalems invoke divine approval for their politics, Bethlehems suffer harm. Which is why Jesus was born in Bethlehem, siding with the crushed-under-foot, subverting narratives of power, representing a different kind of kingdom.

And Jesus' death, at the hands of empire, on a device of State-sanctioned violence, the cross, which was a political symbol for the putting down of rebellion long before it was a religious symbol, demonstrates his solidarity with victims of empire at all times and in all places. Suzanne Watts Henderson speaks of Jesus' death like this:

> For one thing, the cross saves us from the delusion that strength lies in political power exerted coercively over other human beings. Jesus died as he lived: in vulnerable solidarity with human weakness. In life and death he exposed and subverted human

---

4. Ateek, "An Easter Message from Sabeel."

systems—economic, social, political, and religious—that deploy strategies of separation, stratification and violence.[5]

Watts' phrase, "vulnerable solidarity," expresses the power of the doctrine of the incarnation to those who suffer. Jesus is like us! Jesus is one of us! He chose to be born in the wrong place, on the wrong side of history, amongst the wrong kind of people. This choice transforms the world's "wrong" into God's "right." The Bethlehems of the world are precisely where God is working, where God is present, where God chooses to take flesh. And any mission in the name of this God should bear the same character. Mission ought to be incarnational, vulnerable, humble, proximate, intimate. When mission is allied with cultural power, it denies its origins. Bethlehem, solidarity and mission, when inseparable, become insuperable.

JESUS' BIRTH UNDER EMPIRE

Jesus was probably born in 4 BC. We can triangulate his birth from Luke's information, Herod's death (Matt 2:19) and the start of John the Baptist's ministry (Luke 3:1–2). Unfortunately, when in AD 525 Pope John I commissioned a monk called Dionysius to prepare a standard calendar for the church, starting from the date of Jesus' birth, Dionysius set AD 1 as Rome's seven hundred and fifty-third year—and he was out by about four years.

When Joseph and Mary arrived in Bethlehem, it was a building-site. Herod the Great, *not* from the lineage of David, *not* from the tribe of Judah, was Rome's vassal king, and Herod loved building. Casting himself as a new Solomon, Herod was building an unsustainably, unaccountably large temple in Jerusalem. This temple, he hoped, would boost the economy, stamp his ego physically on the nation, and afford him some control through his patronage of the religious elite. To solve the water problem in Jerusalem, Herod was employing Roman technology to bring water via a brand-new aqueduct from Bethlehem. Everything about Herod's Jerusalem project was a collaboration with the Roman Empire, an enforcing of their colonial structures, and a celebration of concentrated power.[6]

In addition, Herod's monstrous man-made-mountain-vanity-project Herodion was also under construction. Located in the Judean wilderness just outside Bethlehem, Herodion was essentially an artificial mountain,

---

5. Raheb & Henderson, *The Cross in Contexts*, 37.

6. Horsley, "Jesus and Empire," 80.

replete with military garrison and extravagant gardens, and it was huge![7] Thirsty for labour, thirsty for precious water, a classic example of imperial architectural arrogance. Bethlehem's people would not have been happy with this state of affairs. Their precious water siphoned off, their young men conscripted for labour: Herod, never popular, was certainly not winning any new friends at this time.[8] "On their way to Bethlehem, Mary and Joseph probably would have seen it in its majesty, poor travellers viewing the pomp of the powerful, and imagining the lavish banquets consumed there."[9]

The village (proudly called "City of David" by the locals, as Luke shows us in 2:4), would still have been comprised of relatives of Joseph, descendants of David. Their ancestors built this village, and they were still here. Not royalty these days, no wealth at all, really, but one can imagine them muttering about Herod the Usurper, praying for a Davidic Messiah, still feeling themselves to be the carriers of the Seed-promise. Joseph and Mary, arriving in the village, would almost certainly have lodged with extended family. There is no scenario wherein a descendant of David would not have been offered hospitality in his ancestral village. "No place for them in the inn" (2:7) is the most notorious English mis-translation of Scripture, where *katalyma* means guest room (as translated in Luke 22:11); the ordinary Greek word for commercial inn, *pandocheion* (as used by Luke in the Good Samaritan parable (10:34)), being clearly *not* used. Joseph and Mary must have been taken into a family home and, the guest-space being already full, have been given a sleeping-space at the animal end of the house, people normally keeping their livestock with them in the house overnight for warmth and safety.[10] Thompson, a nineteenth century missionary scholar, observed such homes in Bethlehem, writing, "It is my impression that the birth actually took place in an ordinary house of some common peasant, and that the baby was laid in one of the mangers, such as are still found in the dwellings of farmers in this region."[11] Many Bethlehem dwellings had a lower floor which was carved out of the soft limestone, keeping the house warm in winter and cool in summer. If indeed Christ was born in the cave-like animal-section of a normal village house, then Luke's account

7. The Arabic name *Jebel Fureidis* means "Paradise Mountain."

8. Josephus, *Jewish War*.

9. Cavicchia, "Fears of the Tyrant," 15.

10. For a fuller discussion see Bailey, *Middle Eastern Eyes*, 25–37.

11. Thompson, *The Land and the Book*, 2:503.

is easily reconciled with the tradition of a cave or grotto as the setting for the Nativity.

The overwhelming impression left by this whole story is one of ordinariness.

Carrying on with the normality of life under empire is a powerful form of resistance. Just carrying on, just surviving, the triumph of the ordinary.

Bethlehem is still a place of protest today. Not so much armed protest, but protest by existing. "We are still here. We are still ourselves. We have outlived many occupations, and we will outlive you." It is mature protest. Resistance by existence. Three thousand five hundred years is a long time to have learnt how to subsist, even to thrive, under occupation, whilst empires have come and gone.[12] Bethlehem is never flamboyant, she keeps her head down, she knows how to be marginal, hers is a hard-won experience, an embattled marginality. She has much to teach.

Even her theology—the modern Palestinian contextual theologies from within the Bethlehemite Protestant community—even her theology is not extravagant. Her theologians keep a quiet dignity. They do make a noise, they do protest, but not by utilising all the machinery of the empire. They protest by preaching the gospel, equipping young Palestinians to make a living, resisting the "brain-drain" that would draw all their intellectual potential off to easier climes. Munther Isaac, Bethlehem-born theologian, writes, in his recent book *The Other Side of the Wall,*

> A theology from behind the wall is concerned with day-to-day issues in Palestine. We are preoccupied with issues of life under occupation, injustice, nonviolence, religious extremism, and peacemaking. We talk about identity and nationality. We do not write theology in libraries; we write it at the checkpoint.[13]

Contemporary Palestinians are leaning into the beauty of the ordinary as resistance. For example, Dr. Abdel Fattah Abusrour, who was born in Aida Refugee Camp in Bethlehem, has written *Bethlehem: Beautiful Resistance Recipes,* a cookbook of traditional Palestinian recipes, with profits going into local community development.

Bethlehem is stubborn, but not bitter. She weeps, but she has always wept. She protests, but not with violence. She endures. She exhibits a resilient meekness. And she retains her dignity. Bethlehem, in this way, is

---

12. The archaeology of Bethlehem suggests the continuity and stability of the local settlement, whilst imperial masters came and went. See Blincoe, *Bethlehem,* 29.

13. Isaac, *The Other Side,* 19.

emblematic of Middle Eastern Christianity, which through generations of humiliations and persecutions has endured, has kept praying and preaching and peace-making.

Of the many slogans graffitied on the wall, one of the most eye-catching reads, "Our revenge will be the laughter of our children." For those subsisting under empire, this statement exhibits the three cardinal virtues of faith, hope and love: faith, believing that the Almighty will arrange a just outcome in due course; hope, symbolised by the laughter of children; and love, in the refusal to exact revenge by violent means.

20

Jesus
The Lamb and the Shepherd

When the angels went away from them into heaven, the shepherds said
to one another, "Let us go over to Bethlehem and see this thing that has
happened, which the Lord has made known to us."

—LUKE 2:15

UP THE HILL TO Bethlehem went the shepherds, with the words of the angels ringing in their ears and in their hearts. Bethlehem is still a shepherds'
town. From time immemorial, the arts of lambing and shearing and slaugh-
tering remain well-developed here. These wilderness-facing highlands
have been, for thousands of years, the summer pastures of semi-nomadic
shepherd communities. During the winter months, when the rainfall turns
the wilderness green, the herdsmen and their families set out with their
tents on their annual itinerations, grazing their flocks across a wide area.
In March or April, when the rain stops, the same communities take to their

settled phase, lambing in the spring and staying close to Bethlehem's water supply through to October or November.[1]

Spending half the year travelling and half the year settled, a lifestyle known as *transhumance*, has its advantages. In the unpredictable Middle Eastern climate, this mixed approach mitigates against risk. If water sources dry up, landed farmers are exposed, whilst nomadic herdsmen can move on to find water elsewhere. Mobility also protects the tribe against tyrannical rulers—it is harder to tax a moving target. This, of course, is what David did under Saul—took to the wilderness which he knew so well as a buffer against an evil king. At most times in history, these semi-nomadic communities in the Near East can be estimated at 10 percent of the total population.[2]

Today, if you visit Bethlehem, a taxi from Manger Square can take you to "The Shepherds' Fields," just out of town to the east, close to the village of Beit Sahour. Beit Sahour, meaning *The House of Staying up All Night* (alluding to Luke 2:8), is said by locals to have been established in the mid-thirteenth century.[3] At the birth of Christ, then, it was just fields.

Characteristic of the region were stone watchtowers where shepherds could look out over their grazing flocks—you can still see some of these today. Genesis 35:21 tells us that after Rachel was buried, Jacob continued on his journey and grazed his flocks at *Migdal Eder,* the Tower of the Flock. Jerome, when he was based in Bethlehem translating the Bible, confirmed this location (probably already preserved in local tradition) as the *Migdal Eder* of both Genesis 35:21 and Micah 4:8, which reads:

> And you, O tower of the flock, hill of the daughter of Zion, to you shall it come, the former dominion shall come, kingship for the daughter of Jerusalem.

The Targums, commenting on Genesis 35:21 declare that the fields visited by Jacob would be the place where the messianic king would be revealed. Again, this derives from the understanding that if a place is mentioned by name in Scripture, it is theologically significant. The place names in the Bible are not just there to help with navigation. Geography is a vehicle for theology. These same fields, visited by the shepherd-father of the nation, the first one to call God "Shepherd," frequented by David as a child,

---

1. Gottwald, *Tribes,* 437. Seale, *Desert Bible,* 75.

2. Gottwald, *Tribes,* 443.

3. Raheb & Strickert, *Bethlehem 2000,* 59.

are the natural location for the angelic announcement of the long-awaited Messiah. Indeed, this announcement could not have happened anywhere else.

In the days of Herod the Great, its proximity to Jerusalem meant that lambs born in Bethlehem were later taken into Jerusalem to be sold as sacrifices for Passover. The Mishnah confirms that sheep for temple-sacrifice were grazed at Migdal Eder, in the Bethlehem environs.[4]

Jerusalem, with no natural advantages, was built almost entirely on pilgrimage. Holiness was good business. Her crowded, cramped, at times claustrophobic streets welcomed the faithful all year round, and especially on feast days. And at the centre of its economy stood Herod's brand-new gleaming temple, dominating the cityscape. The temple was hungry for the meat of sacrificed animals, thirsty for blood. Thousands of lambs would be reared in the vicinity to be killed. The scale of the enterprise was spiralling rapidly out of control. Injustice inevitably follows on the heels of power. Bethlehem was one of the feeder towns for this insatiable beast.

Lambs, born in Bethlehem, the House of Meat, were slaughtered in Jerusalem. And tonight, the Lamb of God is born in Bethlehem. The Lamb of God, born in Bethlehem, destined for slaughter by the temple elite. God's solidarity with victims. God's empathy with the oppressed. God's presence in the margins.

When the angelic choir were practicing in heaven, one can imagine a young angel chorister addressing Gabriel: "Father Gabriel, sir. To whom will we be performing? To kings? To great crowds? In a mighty city theatre?" "No," says Gabriel, "to shepherds on the night shift, in a tiny village, in the margins of the world."

In Scripture, angels often appear in the desert, in the wide-open spaces, away from civilisation. In Scripture, angels often speak to the tired, the disempowered, the poor. Abused Hagar, Manoah's barren wife, hounded Elijah. And now, angels appear to shepherds.

Shepherds were among the most despised of tradespeople. The uneasy relationship between settled crop-growers and nomadic livestock herders is as old as the hills. They compete for the same primary resource—the soil's fertility. Ever since Abel, who was looked down on by his brother the farmer, shepherds have been seen by settled land-owners as inferior. All they do is sit and watch the sheep destroy the winter growth—even the village idiot could do that! Landed Cain, ("the Producer") despised landless

4. *Shekalim* 7:4.

Abel ("the Meaningless/the Breath") and was incensed when God valued Abel's offering and not his own. David, the Overlooked, the Superfluous, was disregarded by his older brothers. As the youngest, he was consigned to Bethlehem's fields. Yet God chose him over his brothers. God chose the shepherd.

In Jesus' time, Rabbis considered shepherds unclean. For example, they were ineligible to be judges or witnesses, as they were considered dishonest.[5] They are a prime example of a disempowered, marginal community. Yet God was pleased to be known as the Shepherd of his people, and now the Good Shepherd is born. "It seems," writes Anyabwile, "that God believes high theology should be given to low people."[6]

Remember Bethlehem's Arabic name? *Beyt Laham*: House of Meat—specifically mutton. It is possible that this derives from an older Aramaic homonym, *Beit Lamra*—the House of Lamb.[7] The shepherds receiving the angelic announcement were semi-nomadic, Arabs or proto-Arabs like the Idumeans who lived in nearby Hebron, ancestors of the Bedouin today. Proximity to the Dead Sea with its chemical composition made Bethlehem a centre for many of the processes associated with wool: cleaning, fulling, dying. Fulling also required access to large amounts of water, not available for miles around but plentiful in Bethlehem. It is easy to imagine semi-nomadic Arab shepherds, bringing their sheep up from the wilderness, using Bethlehem as a summer pasture, a processing plant and a gateway to the ravenous religious market in Jerusalem. It is appropriate to infer that the shepherds were Arab.

The House of Meat becomes the place of word-become-meat, the place of *in-carn-ation*.

> Not friends and family, but strangers. Nomadic shepherds, considered untrustworthy as they lived in the hills and were constantly on the move. They were regarded as unclean, too, carrying the stench of sheep and sleeping rough. But God sends angels to invite these homeless strangers to welcome his homeless son into the world.[8]

So tonight, there is an insignificant village, and the least esteemed of citizens—outsiders, even—and the skies lit up with multitudes of angels singing "Glory to God in the highest!" The shepherds rush to see this thing

5. *Sanhedrin* 25b.

6. Anyabwile, *Luke*, 43.

7. Blincoe, *Bethlehem*, 7.

8. Kandiah, *God is Stranger*, Kindle Location 3321.

that has happened, and they are among the first to behold the Good Shepherd. Jesus, Lamb of God and God's anointed Shepherd. Born in Bethlehem, home of lambs and shepherds.

Swaddling cloths were for wrapping around new-born lambs, to preserve their delicate skins from spot or blemish, to increase their value at Passover. Moses had commanded that Passover lambs be spotless. Joseph and Mary took these up and swaddled the Christ-child. What a sign! Born is the Lamb of God, swaddled and spotless. Born is the Lamb, in Bethlehem, town of shepherds. Born is the Lamb, on his way to Jerusalem as a Paschal sacrifice.

Born is the Shepherd. Born is the Lamb.

21

Epilogue
Woman, Child, Snake, Seed

She gave birth to a male child, one who is to rule all the nations with a rod
of iron, but her child was caught up to God and to his throne,
  and the woman fled into the wilderness, where she has a place prepared by God, in which she is to be nourished for 1,260 days.

—REVELATION 12:5–6

MANSAF IS A TRADITIONAL Palestinian-Bedouin dish of slow-cooked
lamb in fermented yoghurt, with other strong flavours such as cardamom,
allspice, cinnamon and pine nuts. It is a special, celebratory food, not an
everyday food, and requires a certain palate to appreciate the overpowering
mix of flavours. Revelation 12 is like *mansaf.* A disproportionate number
of the leading words and key themes that we have followed throughout
the Bethlehem story are densely packed into these verses, its flavours are
extreme, its colours bright. Like handfuls of spices tossed into a big pot, so
in this chapter we encounter the child, a woman in labour and giving birth,
a snake grown into a dragon, a shepherd with a kingdom that includes all

nations, the wilderness as a place of refuge, the Seed being persecuted by the Snake, and salvation through a sacrificial lamb.

Revelation 12 is a version of the Christmas story not often read at Christmas. In this chapter, the Bethlehem story, the whole macro-narrative of the cosmos, is retrospectively retold. Eugene Peterson calls it a supplement to the traditional Advent readings: "It is St. John's Spirit-appointed task to supplement the work of St. Matthew and St. Luke so that the nativity cannot be sentimentalized into coziness, nor domesticated into drabness, nor commercialized into worldliness."[1]

With so many of our key words recurring here, and so many significant subplots finding resolution here, it is important that we finish our journey, which began in Genesis 3:15, in this chapter, taking our leading words in hand one at a time in order to reflect on their development.

THE CHILD

Ever since Eve, we have been waiting for a snake-slaying man-child. Isaiah's innovation was that the seed of the woman would be an infant, representing the triumph of innocence and the weak shaming the strong.

This trope was widespread across ancient mythologies—an evil usurper who is doomed to be vanquished by a yet unborn prince. The usurper tries to kill the pregnant mother before she can bring the saviour to birth. The baby is born, and slays the monster. In Babylonian mythology, the monster Tiamat is overcome by a youthful Marduk. In Egypt, the serpent Typhon pursues the goddess Isis, who gives birth to Horus, who kills Typhon. In ancient Greece, the evil snake is Python, the mother is Leto, and the baby is Apollo, who at four days old kills the snake. "The parallels to these various myths are too striking to be accidental and too early to argue that they are derived from Revelation. Rather, John has freely drawn on elements of these myths, adding certain elements to conform the story to the Christian narrative about their saviour."[2] This story is as old as the world, sprinkled across the cultures of the Near East. Jesus is the fulfilment of the varied baseline narratives of all peoples.

Various emperors also claimed their divine credentials via these stories. The Rome of John's day had co-opted the Apollo story, and several emperors claimed descent from Apollo. In this way, John, as he does

1. Peterson, *Reversed Thunder*, 121.
2. Witherington, *Revelation*, 165.

throughout Revelation, subverts the imperial story, claiming that Christ, not Caesar, was the true Saviour of the world. Consistent with the Bethlehem story, then, John is taking an anti-empire stance, a prophetic "outsiderness" to prevailing narratives of power. DaSilva explains the impact that this would have had on the scattered, persecuted Christians reading these words: "Revelation offers a de-imperialization of the local Christians' worldview. . . . As John's hearers encounter representations of this story in art, they would begin to view it quite subversively as a reminder of Christ's ascendancy and the monstrous power behind Roman rule."[3]

The child, who is under fire at the point of birth, is Jesus Christ, under fire by Herod immediately he is born. Verse 5 represents a telescoping of the whole of Jesus' life, from his birth through to his ascension, when he is "caught up to the throne of God."

THE WOMAN

Who, then, is the woman who brings him to birth? Consistent with the Bethlehem story, she represents the whole line of individual Messiah-mothers, from Eve to Mary, who have overcome opposition to fulfil the Seed-promise and give birth to boys who will fight dragons. She is also a depiction of the corporate people of God, the Old Testament people of Israel, who become, in the New Testament, the church (Is 66:6–9; Gal 4:26). "She represents the entire story of God's people, chosen to carry forward his plans for the nations and indeed for the whole creation."[4] The mother from whom comes forth the Son. "This woman," writes Witherington, "is a survivor and an exemplar of durability and paradoxically of vulnerability, but the durability comes from the protection God affords, not from any inherent strength."[5] We see in her the grittiness and resourcefulness common to Tamar and Ruth and Mary. She is determined to bring forth Christ.

BIRTHPAINS

John is explicit about the birthpains that the woman experiences.

3. DaSilva, *Seeing Things John's Way*, 104–5.
4. Wright, *Revelation*, Kindle Location 1908.
5. Witherington, *Revelation*, 173.

She was pregnant and was crying out in birth pains and the agony
of giving birth. Revelation 12:2[/EXT}

Right at the beginning, in the *protoevangelium*, Eve was told, "I will
surely multiply your pain in childbearing; in pain you shall bring forth children" (Gen 3:16), and we have followed the pain of mothers throughout
the evolution of Scripture. Rachel's difficult labour resulted in her death
at Bethlehem. Micah prophesied a shepherd, at Bethlehem, "when she
who is in labour has given birth." For Isaiah, labour pains are a common
metaphor for the struggle to bring forth the kingdom of God (Is 26:16–18,
54:1, 66:7–9). Indeed, "in the prophets, birthpains were often the suffering
of foreign captivity and imminent deliverance from foreign oppression."[6]
Bethlehem herself groaned with pain as Christ was born and Herod put her
sons to the sword. Jesus frequently used this expression in an eschatological
sense (Matt 24:8; Mark 13:8; John 16:21). Paul analogised the difficulty of
apostolic ministry as "the anguish of childbirth" (Gal 4:19) and spoke of a
kind of cosmic labour pain as new creation comes forth (Rom 8:22).

The suffering of mothers has been front and centre in this story—the
birthpains of the kingdom, the suffering of those who struggle for justice.
This is more than a message of "no pain, no gain." This is an affirmation that
the pain of God's people, the church, throughout the earth is eschatological, laden with dignity, fraught with meaning. If you are suffering for righteousness' sake, you are blessed! Throughout this book we have stressed
suffering. Persecution and disempowerment are normative for the church,
scattered throughout the Bethlehems of the world.

THE SHEPHERD

The male child will shepherd (*poimenein*) all the nations with a rod of iron
(Rev 12:5). This is a direct allusion to Psalm 2, a messianic psalm in which
shepherd language becomes king language, much as, in David, a shepherd
became a king. In the previous chapter, John had applied that psalm explicitly to Jesus (11:18), as many other New Testament writers have also done.

The humble shepherding emblem *shevet* (staff) promised to Judah in
Genesis 49:10 and again by Balaam in Numbers 24:17,[7] the rod used by

---

6. Beale, *Revelation*, 630.

7. Both Hebrews 1:2 and 2 Peter 1:17–19 combine Psalm 2 and Numbers 24 in
speaking of Jesus.

God himself as shepherd in Psalm 23:4 and 45:6, according to David who understood shepherding, in Psalm 2:9 becomes a rod of iron in the hand of Messiah.[8] In the wisdom literature the *shevet* becomes an instrument of discipline and chastisement, and in Isaiah 11:4, Messiah employs it to bring forth justice. For Micah, the messianic shepherd will use his *shevet* to care for God's end-time flock.

Jesus is the Anointed One of Psalm 2, the international king of Psalm 2, the Son of Psalm 2. He is of Judah, receiving the promised staff/sceptre. He is of David, the shepherd-king from Bethlehem. He inaugurates the promised peace of Isaiah 11. He shepherds the nations. With the *shevet* in his hand, he cares for and disciplines his sheep, and protects them from their enemies.

ALL THE NATIONS

Jesus is the Shepherd, not only of Israel, but of all the nations. A global problem has a global saviour. This international note has sounded throughout the story, from the promise to Abram in Genesis 12, through the prophecies of Micah and Isaiah. The Bethlehem story has had an internationalising default since the beginning; Tamar, Balaam, Rahab, Ruth, Ibzan, the wise men at Jesus' birth. Even should you try and stop the nations coming in, you cannot. Jesus has all the nations in his DNA—he belongs to all people. His birth under empire gives him solidarity with all peoples. He shepherds all nations.

THE DRAGON

> Finally, with a swish of his majestic tail, the villain appears on stage—the villain who, we quickly learn, stands behind all the trouble that we have seen in the earlier chapters. The dark secret is revealed; the real problem is identified; the curtain has risen on the drama-within-the-drama, the central action which forms, now, the central scene in the whole book.[9]

---

8. "Most certainly the phrase "a rod of iron" (Ps 2:9; Rev 2:27; 12:5) refers to the shepherd's rod/mace with heavy pieces of iron driven into its head. . . The instrument itself is about two and a half feet long with a mace-like end into which heavy pieces of iron are often embedded." Bailey, *The Good Shepherd*, 52.

9. Wright, *Revelation*, Kindle Location 1911.

The serpent of Genesis 3:15 has become the dragon of Revelation 12:3. Indeed, snake and dragon are used interchangeably throughout Scripture to depict the devil. They are chaos creatures—unclean, dangerous, evil. More specifically, dragon is frequently a symbol of the devilish power which lies behind evil empires which oppress God's people. Egypt, Babylon, and Rome are all variously identified with the dragon (Ps 73:13–14, 89:10; Is 30:7, 51:9; Ezek 29:3, 32:2–3; Hab 3:8–15; Jer 51:34; Amos 9:3; *Pss. Sol.* 2:29–30). The phrase "the great dragon" (verses 3 and 9) is particularly used of Pharaoh in Ezekiel 29.3.[10]

The seed of the snake, throughout history, has persecuted the seed of the woman. In particular, evil empires have arisen, beginning with Nimrod, with grim, racist ambitions towards world domination, and such powerful control over the dominant narrative that the self-determination of marginal peoples, languages, and identities has been entirely suppressed. One of the great tragedies of world history is when Christian mission has aligned itself with these imperialistic ambitions, rather than siding with those oppressed. John is calling his readers to discern the demonic foundation of their contemporary power, and will we not do the same in our day?

THE LAMB

And how is the great dragon defeated? "They have conquered him by the blood of the lamb" (12.11). Finally, the Lamb of God, born in Bethlehem, the House of Meat, where the patriarch Jacob first grazed his lambs, is offered in victorious sacrifice. Lambs, born in Bethlehem to be sacrificed in Jerusalem at Passover. Passover, when by the blood of lambs the people of God are released from the brutal clutches of the great Egyptian dragon. Behold the Lamb, by whose blood the dragon is finally defeated.

Beginning with Judah, whose self-sacrifice qualified him for kingship, we have seen venom-absorbers voluntarily stamping on snakes, heroically giving up their own lives for the salvation of others. We see Boaz' costly redemption of Ruth, and Joseph's courageous welcome of Mary. In equal measure, we see, in vain attempts to cling on to power, the failed leadership of Saul, Rehoboam and Herod. Vulnerable sacrifice, at the very heart of a Bethlehem-centric faith, is epitomised and immortalised in Jesus Christ, the Lamb of God who takes away the sins of the world, whose death disempowers power, defangs the snake, and liberates the oppressed.

10. Beale, *Revelation*, 632–3.

WILDERNESS

The next weighty, strongly-flavoured word in this passage is "wilderness," which constitutes a God-appointed refuge into which the woman can flee. With undeniable tones of the Exodus, as the people flee Pharaoh into the wilderness, and David, who found refuge there from Saul, wilderness was a hugely important part of Jewish tradition. YHWH is first known as God of mountains and deserts, and his people have often gone back to the desert to find him—a kind of anti-urban empire detox. Many of the first century messianic movements were associated with the desert,[11] not least the Qumran community southeast of Bethlehem where the Judean wilderness meets the Dead Sea.[12] Psalms 23 and 78, which spoke of a table in the wilderness amongst enemies, were understood to be messianic. Here the hospitality of God is on display. When Jesus gives bread to 5,000 in the wilderness, we know him to be Messiah (Mark 6:31).

"Wings" and "wilderness" come together in David's Psalm 55:

> And I say, "Oh, that I had wings like a dove! I would fly away and
> be at rest;
>> yes, I would wander far away; I would lodge in the wilder-
> ness." Psalm 55:6–7

David's habit of "going Bedouin" and fleeing to the Judean wilderness for sanctuary is paradigmatic for Israel. The eagle's wings that carried them into safety from Pharaoh (Ex 19:4; Deut 32:10–11) are replaced for David by doves' wings and refuge from Saul. Elijah fled for fear of Jezebel back to the wilderness in order to hear the voice of God once again. The prophets saw rescue from exile in Babylon as being an Exodus-like rescue through the wilderness towards the promised land (Is 40:3; Jer 31:2; Hos 2:14).

Jesus, like Israel in its truest form, is tempted and protected in the wilderness. Like David and Elijah, he flees to the wilderness when persecuted (John 11:53, 54).

Amongst early Christians, the desert fathers would do exactly this, fleeing the Babylons of their day, responding to the urgent command, "Come out of her, my people, lest you take part in her sins" (Rev 18:4). Unveiling the evil undergirding worldly systems was a key purpose of apocalyptic literature. This call to be counter-cultural has never gone away.

---

11. Josephus frequently identified messianic movements with desert and exodus themes, *J.W* 2.259–62; 7.438; *Ant* 20.168–72.

12. 1QM 1.2–3; 1QS 8.12–15, 9.18–21.

Wilderness was always supposed to be an antidote to wealth and power (Deut 8:14–17).

Three and a half years (forty-two months or 1,260 days) is a symbolic number for a partial time of testing with an end in sight. Where seven years is total, three and half years is partial. This is the length of Elijah's drought (Luke 4:25), the length of time prophesied by Daniel (in chapters 7, 9 and 12), but also brings to mind Israel's forty-two years in the wilderness (Num 33:5–49). It will not be forever. But as long as this pressure lasts, the desert will keep God's people safe.

THE SEED

Finally, we come to the final use of the word "seed" in Scripture (verse 17), and we discover that the Seed, which has been the corporate people of God and, ultimately, Jesus himself, is now us, those who are in Christ. We learn that the Seed is "those who keep the commandments of God and hold to the testimony of Jesus." This story is our story! Genesis 3:15 spoke of enmity between the serpent and the woman, and between the seed of the serpent and the seed of the woman. Revelation 12 depicts the conflict between snake and woman, and Revelation 13 between the serpent's seed and the woman's seed.

Undeniably, in Revelation, empire is identified with evil, an enemy of the faithful. A line is drawn through Babylon (taking us back to Nimrod, the first tyrannical emperor, enemy of Abram), to Egypt (Pharaoh as "the great dragon," and the Exodus as the great paradigm of rescue) to contemporary Rome. The positionality of Bethlehem, marginal to empire and victim of such totalising systems, epitomises Christian resistance to the status quo in every generation. Palestinian Christian non-violent resistance to empire in their context is paradigmatic for all Christ-followers in all generations. We are called to flee to the metaphorical wilderness, to discern the dragon behind the systems of our time, to align with prophetic critique of prevailing narratives. Witherington's reflection on Revelation 12 gathers these threads together:

> A stance of passive resistance or even of nonresistance is nonetheless a profoundly political posture and act. It is not quietism or a retreat into mysticism; it is a way of saying no to the demands

of the powers and principalities, no to idolatry and immorality, without resorting to the tactics of one's opponents.[13]

Jesus' birth through vulnerability and suffering is an act of spiritual warfare, an active resistance. It is anti-empire, subverting narratives of power, with flight to the wilderness and lamb-slaughter being how the snake is overthrown. Christmas is battle. Bethlehem a battlefield. And the weapons of warfare are labour pains, lament, suffering and martyrdom. What looks like defeat is victory. And Jesus, the Child, the undefeated, the Shepherd, the bearer of the staff-scepter, of the tribe of Judah and the village of Bethlehem, the slayer of the dragon and the protector of his people, is Lord and King and Saviour. Halleluiah. Amen.

13. Witherington, *Revelation*, 174.

Afterword
by David Devenish

I HAVE VERY MUCH appreciated my friendship with Andy McCullough as we have served together over many years. I felt blessed then when Andy sent me a draft of his new book, *The Bethlehem Story: Mission and Justice in the Margins of the World*. Having read through it and made a few comments to him, I added that I felt it needed a short chapter of application together with a summary of lessons for us in the church of Jesus Christ today. Andy thought about this and then said to me, "Will you write it?" I found this humbling and a challenge but also a privilege.

In chapter 13, Andy refers to the prophetic nature of the story of Bethlehem for the church's mission; "Mission is at its best when it is prophetic. Prophecy is at best when it is missional." What I am attempting to do in this afterword is select a small number of what I believe will prove to be prophetic applications from this great story.

LESSONS FOR CHRISTIAN LEADERS

Firstly, in this story of little Bethlehem, there are important lessons for the style of leadership to be demonstrated in the church today. Bethlehem speaks of humility; "But you, O Bethlehem Ephrathah, are only a small village among all the people of Judah. Yet a ruler of Israel, whose origins are in the distant past, will come from you on my behalf" (Micah 5:2, NLT). David was anointed in a small, insignificant village, as the youngest in the family who was not even invited to the feast. In the same way, the promised ruler that came from Bethlehem was meek and lowly in heart, came as one who served rather than to be served, stooped to wash his disciples' feet. Even beyond Bethlehem, it is significant that he was brought up in

Nazareth where "nothing good could come from" according to the understanding of the people of that day. Christian leadership today is so success orientated, methods are taught to help us achieve "leadership success." The Biblical way of success is the way of stooping, serving, a willingness to be "unknown, and yet well known" (2 Corinthians 6:9). It is cross-centred, servant leadership that lives out the message of the foolishness of the cross as well as teaching it. It is being willing to serve even if we don't achieve any fame. Bethlehem in Scripture is like that and yet today the "little town" is celebrated all over the world because of who was born there.

Secondly, there is a further lesson for Christian leaders today in the contrast that Andy draws between Bethlehem and Jerusalem. So often Jerusalem was the place of moral failure, as in the case of both David and Solomon, and was the place from which, because of national sin, the glory was seen to depart (Ezekiel 10). It was where the enemies of Jesus' ministry, both political and religious, were gathered. Like many preachers, I have often taught that it was when David had settled down that he fell into sin with Bathsheba. Previously, however, I had not seen the significance of the fact that it was also after he had come to the position of power in Jerusalem rather than the position of humility represented by Bethlehem and by his "Bedouin like" wanderings in the wilderness around Bethlehem. I believe this is so true today. Christian leadership can fail morally or by abusing authority (Solomon fell in both) when it achieves a position of power rather than a position of ongoing dependence and servanthood. I have frequently wondered why the motif of "shepherds" was used to describe the leaders in Israel when the shepherds were often, as were those in the hills around Bethlehem, the despised of society. I believe there is a lesson for us in this, to emphasise not only the shepherds' care of the sheep but also their relative unimportance religiously and culturally. Let us remain leaders content to serve and care, and cherish our cultural unimportance!

CHALLENGES TO PREJUDICE IN THE CHURCH

Another clear lesson that Bethlehem teaches us is that, sadly, throughout its history, the church has often identified itself with nationalism, racial prejudice and imperialism. This is still an issue today. Any sense of national superiority is inimical to the gospel for all nations (Colossians 3:11). The welcome and honour given to the outsider —whether Rahab, Ruth the Moabitess, or the Magi from the East—are all characteristics of Bethlehem.

By contrast, in Jerusalem, the other nations were excluded from the inner parts of the Temple. A challenge for all our churches is how we welcome those from different ethnic or social backgrounds and incorporate them fully into every level of church life.

Similarly, our mission is to be to all, including—even particularly—those at the margins of society, like the shepherds and others who benefitted from the hospitality of Bethlehem. Sometimes there can be a focus in our mission on people of influence and, of course, they are to be reached by the gospel too. Boaz was a wealthy man of influence in Bethlehem but what he was commended for was his kindness to the widow and the foreigner. It was this that demonstrated the blessing of God upon his life, the gracious overflow of these blessings to others. Even the "son of peace" (Luke 10:6) who gives entrance for the gospel into a particular context is not necessarily the obviously influential (but can be a lone woman sitting by a well, as in Samaria in John 4).

Connected with this is the fact that respect and honour are to be given to all within the church but with a particular emphasis on those displaced and rejected in the world. Paul writes, "So God has put the body together so that extra honour and care are given to those parts that have less dignity" (1 Corinthians 12:24, NLT). The church is to be the place where the poor are honoured, not just cared for. The refugee is similarly honoured and not just protected, just as Ruth and Rahab were honoured by being joined to the lineage of the Messiah, just as Tamar was respected as being "more righteous." This then is so contrary to the spirit of our "celebrity" church age. Many would teach the need to "honour the pastor." Yes, but equally honour those who have "less dignity" humanly speaking.

LISTENING TO VOICES FROM SOUTH AND EAST

Furthermore, the Western church in particular must learn to listen to those that they would regard as at the margins, or may have never even heard about! As has been frequently documented, the centre of Christianity has moved from the West to the East and the South. However, the Western church, and in particular, Western church leadership must learn to listen to the challenges and understandings and increasingly respect the voices emerging from East and South. They have so much to teach us. The growth of Christianity is occurring with leadership given by many unsung heroes of faith—often persecuted, often despised—rather than from the "celebrities" of the Western church. Bethlehem teaches us the importance of this.

MISSIONARY STRATEGY

Another learning point for our missionary strategy is that we must find the stories and literature within the culture that we are reaching that can point to the coming of the Messiah. The possibility that the Magi looking for a star arose because of the veneration in the East of Balaam's prophecy was a completely new idea to me. However, there are lessons in the book of Acts that help us on this. When Paul preaches to Jews in the Synagogue, he demonstrates that the Old Testament promises are fulfilled in the Messiah. When he addresses the pagans of Athens, he quotes Greek poetry and Athenian heritage stories and applies them to the coming of Christ! How this has happened frequently in the history of world mission is well documented by Don Richardson in his book *Eternity in Their Hearts*. When engaged in mission, we must learn the wisdom distributed by God in his common grace into all cultures, and show how the fulfilment of all their hopes and desires as expressed in their literature is found in the Messiah from Bethlehem.

APPRECIATION OF BIBLICAL THEOLOGY

Reading a book like this underlines the need for us to appreciate Biblical theology as well as systematic theology. Some of my friends from the East tell me that Westerners often just take part of a story rather than tracing the story to its origins. This leads to us failing to fully understand the story. Andy's study of Bethlehem corrects that tendency, enabling us to understand the overall story of God's purposes fulfilled in a way that brings down the proud and exalts the lowly (Luke 1:51–52).

There remains a God-given desire for fulfilment of the promises in Scripture for Jerusalem. Jerusalem or Zion was expressed in the longings of Old Testament poets and the hopes of Old Testament prophets. These hopes were fulfilled in Christ and are now also demonstrated in the church of Jesus Christ, composed of Jew and Gentile who have already come to "mount Zion . . . the city of the living God, the heavenly Jerusalem" (Hebrews 12:22). Our longing, however, is still for the future fulness of the New Jerusalem which comes down to earth after Jesus returns and ushers in the age of the new heaven and new earth. Let us retain the hope of "Jerusalem above" in our hearts, whilst living out our corporate church life, leadership and mission according to the example of Bethlehem.

Like the story of the seed, we are small and humble, yet bless the nations of the world. It is the way of the Kingdom, the way God's promises of blessing are fulfilled. Bethlehem's story teaches us this; let us serve God and engage in mission in God's way represented by Bethlehem, not man's way of arrogance and celebrity.

My wife, Scilla, and I had the privilege of being in Bethlehem shortly before Christmas a few years ago with other church leaders as guests of Bethlehem Bible College. We noticed along the street a Christmas tree on which all the baubles were spent tear gas canisters. In Bethlehem we see the beginning of the promise—that the peace of God will come, bread will be provided to the nations and eventually swords will be turned into plough-shares as the nations flow to the mountain of the Lord—now fulfilled in Jesus Christ. Let us keep this hope in our hearts.

David Devenish led the Newfrontiers Together Team from 2012 until October 2020. He has served in church planting mission in different parts of the world and has authored several books.

Bibliography

Addison, Stephen. *Movements that Change the World: Five Keys to Spreading the Gospel.* Smyrna: Missional Press, 2009. Kindle Edition.

Allen, Leslie C. *Books of Joel, Obadiah, Jonah and Micah (New International Commentary on the Old Testament).* Grand Rapids: Eerdmans, 1976.

Alter, Robert. *The Art of Biblical Narrative. Revised and Updated.* New York: Basic, 2011. Kindle Edition.

———. *The Five Books of Moses (The Hebrew Bible: A Translation with Commentary).* New York: Norton, 2019.

———. *Prophets (The Hebrew Bible: A Translation with Commentary).* New York: Norton, 2019.

Anyabwile, Thabiti. *Exalting Jesus in Luke (Christ-Centred Exposition).* Nashville: B&H, 2018.

Ateek, Naim Stifan. "An Easter Message from Sabeel" (Sabeel, 2001). https://web.archive.org/web/20080310035855/http://www.sabeel.org/old/reports/easter01.htm

———. *Justice and Only Justice: A Palestinian Theology of Liberation.* New York: Orbis, 1989.

Bailey, Kenneth E. *Finding the Lost: Cultural Keys to Luke 15.* St. Louis: Concordia Press, 1992.

———. *Jesus through Middle Eastern Eyes: Cultural Studies in the Gospels.* London: SPCK, 2008.

———. *The Good Shepherd: A Thousand-Year Journey from Psalm 23 to the New Testament.* Downers Grove: IVP, 2014.

Beale, G. K. *A New Testament Biblical Theology: The Unfolding of the Old Testament in the New.* Grand Rapids: Baker Academic, 2011.

———. *The Book of Revelation. The New International Greek Testament Commentary.* Grand Rapids: Eerdmans, 1999.

Blincoe, Nicholas. *Bethlehem: Biography of a Town.* London: Constable, 2017.

Bowmann, Glenn. "A Weeping on the Road to Bethlehem: Contestation over the Uses of Rachel's Tomb." In *Bethlehem: A Sociocultural History,* edited by Mitri Raheb, 165–188. Bethlehem: Diyar, 2020.

Brown, Raymond E. *The Birth of the Messiah: A Commentary on the Infancy Narratives in Matthew and Luke.* New York: Image Books, 1979.

Brueggemann, Walter. *Interrupting Silence: God's Command to Speak Out.* London: Hodder & Stoughton, 2018.

―――. *A Commentary on Jeremiah: Exile & Homecoming.* Grand Rapids: Eerdmans, 1998.

―――. *The Prophetic Imagination. 40th Anniversary Edition.* Minneapolis: Fortress, 2018. Kindle Edition.

Bull, Geoffrey, T. *Love Song in Harvest: An Interpretation of the Book of Ruth.* Glasgow: Pickering & Inglis, 1972.

Bultmann, Rudolph. "ελεος: The OT and Jewish Usage." In *Theological Dictionary of the New Testament,* edited by Gerhard Kittel and G. Friedrich, 2:479. Grand Rapids: Eerdmans, 1964.

Butler, Trent. *Judges (Word Biblical Commentary).* Nashville: Thomas Nelson, 2009.

Caiger, Stephen L. *Lives of the Prophets: A Thousand Years of Hebrew Prophecy Reviewed in its Historical Context.* London: SPCK, 1949.

Cavicchia, Alessandro. "The Fears of the Tyrant and the Trust of the Child," *The Holy Land Review* 12, no. 1 (2018): 15–19.

Cragg, Kenneth. *The Order of the Wounded Hands: Schooled in the East.* London: Melisende, 2006.

Crook, Zeba A. "Reciprocity: Covenantal Exchange as a Test Case." In *Ancient Israel: The Old Testament in its Social Context,* edited by Philip F. Esler, 78–91. London: SCM, 2005.

Dalrymple, William. *From the Holy Mountain: A Journey in the Shadow of Byzantium.* London: Harper, 2011.

daSilva, David A. *Seeing Things John's Way: The Rhetoric of the Book of Revelation.* Louisville, KY: Westminster John Knox, 2000.

Dempster, Stephen G. *Dominon and Dynasty: A Theology of the Hebrew Bible (New Studies in Biblical Theology).* Nottingham: Apollos, 2003.

Dussell, Enrique. *Ethics of Liberation in the Age of Globalization and Exclusion.* Durham: Duke University Press, 2013.

el Saadawi, Nawal. *The Innocence of the Devil.* Translated by Sherif Hetata. London: Methuen, 1994.

Eriksen, Amy J. and Andrew R. Davis. "Recent Research on the Megilloth (Song of Songs, Ruth, Lamentations, Ecclesiastes, Esther)," *Currents in Biblical Research* 14, no.3 (2016) 298–318.

Exum, J. Cheryl. *Fragmented Women: Feminist (Sub)versions of Biblical Narratives.* London: T&T Clark, 2016. Kindle Edition.

Frymer-Kensky, Tikva. *Reading the Women of the Bible: A New Interpretation of their Stories.* New York: Schocken Books, 2002.

―――. "Virginity in the Bible." In *Gender and Law in the Hebrew Bible and the Ancient Near East,* edited by Bernard M. Levinson, Tikva Frymer-Kensky and Victor H. Matthews, 79–96. Sheffield Academic Press, 1998.

Gottwald, Norman K. *The Tribes of Yahweh.* Maryknoll, NY: Orbis, 1979.

Halpern, Baruch. *David's Secret Demons: Messiah, Murderer, Traitor, King.* Grand Rapids: Eerdmans, 2001.

Heschel, Abraham J. *The Prophets.* New York: Harper, 1962.

Hilal, Shireen, "Blessed are the Peacemakers: A Personal Journey." *Bethlehem Bible College* (9 July 2018). https://christatthecheckpoint.bethbc.edu/2018-videos/?page-video09898=1#/lightbox&slide=15

Holdsworth, Stuart. "Cakes Stencils the artist creating a playground on the West Bank Barrier." *Inspiring City* (22 March 2019). https://inspiringcity.com/2019/03/22/an-interview-with-cakes-stencils-the-artist-creating-a-playground-on-the-west-bank-barrier/

Horsley, Richard A. "Jesus and Empire." In *In the Shadow of Empire: Reclaiming the Bible as a History of Faithful Resistance*, edited by Richard A. Horsley, 75–96. Louisville, KY: Westminster John Knox, 2008.

House, Paul R. *Old Testament Theology*. Downer's Grove: IVP Academic, 1998.

Isaac, Munther. "Reading the Old Testament in a Palestinian Church Today: A Case Study of Joshua 6." In *The Land Cries Out: Theology of the Land in the Israeli-Palestinian Context*, edited by Salim J. Munayer and Lisa Loden, 217–233. Eugene, OR: Wipf and Stock, 2012.

———. *The Other Side of the Wall: A Palestinian Christian Narrative of Lament and Hope*. Downer's Grove: IVP, 2020.

Israel, Alex. *I Kings: Torn in Two (Maggid Studies in Tanakh)*. Jerusalem: Koren, 2013. Kindle Edition.

Japhet, Sara, *I & II Chronicles, A Commentary (The Old Testament Library)*. London: SCM, 1993.

Jenkins, Philip. *The New Faces of Christianity: Believing the Bible in the Global South*. Oxford University Press, 2006.

Kandiah, Krish. *God Is Stranger: What Happens When God Turns Up?* London: Hodder & Stoughton, 2017. Kindle Edition.

Katanacho, Yohanna. "Palestinian Orthopathos: Suffering for the Sake of Love, Justice and Peace." *Bethlehem Bible College* (10 July 2018). https://christatthecheckpoint.bethbc.edu/2018-videos/#/lightbox&slide=11

———. *The Land of Christ: A Palestinian Cry*. Eugene, OR: Wipf and Stock, 2013.

Kedourie, Elie. "Introduction." In *The Jewish World: Revelation, Prophecy and History (The Great Civilisations Series)*, edited by Elie Kedourie, 7–52. London: Thames and Hudson, 1979.

Keller, Werner. *The Bible as History: Archaeology Confirms the Book of Books*. Translated by William Neil. London: Hodder and Stoughton, 1956.

Kessler, R. "From Bipolar to Multipolar Understanding: Hermeneutical Consequences of Intercultural Bible Reading." In *Through the Eyes of Another: Intercultural Reading of the Bible*, edited by Hans de Wit, Louis C. Jonker and Daniel S. Schipani, 451–459. Indiana: Institute of Mennonite Studies, 2005.

Kling, Fritz *The Meeting of the Waters. Seven Currents that Will Propel the Future Church*. Colorado Springs: David C. Cook, 2010.

Lau, Peter H. W. *Identity and Ethics in the Book of Ruth: A Social Identity Approach*. Berlin: De Gruyter, 2011.

Lau, Peter H. W. and Gregory Goswell. *Unceasing Kindness: A Biblical Theology of Ruth*. London: Apollos, 2016.

Layton, Scott C. "Whence Comes Balaam? Num. 22:5 Revisited." *Biblica*, 73, no. 1 (1992) 32–61.

Leithart, Peter J. *1 & 2 Chronicles (Brazos Theological Commentary on the Bible)*. Grand Rapids: Baker, 2019.

———. *A House for my Name: A Survey of the Old Testament*. Moscow, ID: Canon, 2000.

———. *A Son to Me: An Exposition of 1&2 Samuel*. Moscow, ID: Canon, 2003.

Lemche, Niels Peter. *The Old Testament Between Theology and History: A Critical Survey*. Louisville, KY: Westminster John Knox, 2008.

Luke, J. T. *Pastoralism and Politics in the Mari Period: A Re-examination of the Character and Political Significance of the Major West Semitic Tribal Groups in the Middle Euphrates.* Ann Arbor: University Microfilms, 1965.

MacArthur, John. *Twelve Extraordinary Women: How God Shaped Women of the Bible and What He Wants to Do With You.* Nashville: Thomas Nelson, 2005.

Malina, Bruce J. *The New Testament World: Insights from Cultural Anthropology.* Rev. ed. Louisville, KY: Westminster John Knox, 1993.

Marteijn, Elizabeth. "Saint, Liberator, Martyr: Popular Palestinian Saint George Veneration in the Village of Al-Khader," in Mitri Raheb (ed.) *Bethlehem: A Sociocultural History,* 81–96. Bethlehem: Diyar, 2020.

Masterman, E. W. G. "The Water Supply of Jerusalem: Ancient and Modern." *The Biblical World* 19, no. 2 (1902) 87–112.

Matthews, Victor H. *The Cultural World of the Bible: An Illustrated Guide to Manners and Customs.* Fourth Edition. Baker Academic: Grand Rapids, 2015.

———. "Honor and Shame in Gender-Related Legal Situations in the Hebrew Bible." In *Gender and Law in the Hebrew Bible and the Ancient Near East,* edited by Bernard M. Levinson, Tikva Frymer-Kensky and Victor H. Matthews, 97–112. Sheffield Academic Press, 1998.

McCullough, Andrew. "Boaz' Bravery: How do the Dynamics of Honour and Shame Contribute to an Understanding of the Costliness of Boaz' Redemption of Ruth, with Specific Reference to Turkish Perspective?" A Dissertation Submitted in Partial Fulfilment of the Requirements for the Degree MTh in Contextual Theology with Mission. All Nations Christian College, 2019.

———. *Global Humility: Attitudes for Mission.* Welwyn Garden City: Malcolm Down, 2017.

Merill, Eugene H. *Kingdom of Priests: A History of Old Testament Israel. Second Edition.* Grand Rapids: Baker, 2008.

Mishra, Pankaj. *From the Ruins of Empire: The Revolt Against the West and the Remaking of Asia.* London: Penguin, 2012.

Moberly, R. W. L. *Old Testament Theology: Reading the Hebrew Bible as Christian Scripture.* Grand Rapids: Baker Academic 2013. Kindle Edition.

Morrison, Craig, E. *2 Samuel (Berit Olam: Studies in Hebrew Narrative and Poetry).* Collegeville, MN: Liturgical, 2013.

Mounce, William D. *The Analytical Lexicon to the Greek New Testament.* Grand Rapids: Zondervan, 1993.

Muilenburg, James. *The Way of Israel: Biblical Faith and Ethics.* New York: Harper, 1961.

Munayer, Salim J. and Lisa Loden, eds. *The Land Cries Out: Theology of the Land in the Israeli-Palestinian Context.* Eugene, OR: Wipf and Stock, 2012.

Munayer, Salim J. "Theology of the Land: From a Land of Strife to a Land of Reconciliation." In *The Land Cries Out: Theology of the Land in the Israeli-Palestinian Context,* edited by Salim J. Munayer and Lisa Loden, 234–264. Eugene, OR: Wipf and Stock, 2012.

Musk, Bill A. *Touching the Soul of Islam: Sharing the Gospel in Muslim Cultures.* Crowborough: Monarch Publications, 1995.

Neyrey, Jerome H. *Honor and Shame in the Gospel of Matthew.* Louisville, KY: Westminster John Knox, 1998.

Nigro, Lorenzo. "Bethlehem in the Bronze and Iron Ages in the Light of Recent Discoveries by the Palestinian Mota-Dach," *Vicino Oriente* XIX (2015): 1–24.

Niles, Daniel Thambyrajah. *This Jesus . . . Whereof We are Witnesses.* Philadelphia: Westminster, 1965.

———. *Upon the Earth: The Mission of God and the Missionary Enterprise of the Churches.* London: Lutterworth, 1962.

O'Brien, Julia M. "Early Christian Interpretation of Micah 4–5." In *Micah (Wisdom Commentary)* edited by Julia M. O'Brien, 60–66. Collegeville, MN: Liturgical, 2017.

Padilla, C. Rene. *Mission Between the Times: Essays on the Kingdom.* Grand Rapids: Eerdmans, 1985.

Padilla DeBorst, Ruth. "Community and Just Conviviality." *A Rocha* (30 June 2020). https://blog.arocha.org/en/community-and-just-conviviality/

Peterson, Eugene H. *Reversed Thunder: The Revelation of John and the Praying Imagination.* New York: HarperCollins, 2011.

Petrotta, Anthony J. "A Closer Look at Matt 2:6 and its Old Testament Sources." *Journal of the Evangelical Theological Society* 28, no.1 (1985) 47–52.

Phipps, Alison. *Decolonising Multilingualism: Struggles to Decreate.* Bristol: Multilingual Matters, 2019.

Pitre, Brant James. *Jesus and the Jewish Roots of Mary: Unveiling the Mother of the Messiah.* New York: Image, 2018.

Raheb, Mitri. "Christmas Eve Sermon." (13 January 2017) https://www.mitriraheb.org/en/article/1484299023

———. *Faith in the Face of Empire: The Bible through Palestinian Eyes.* New York: Orbis, 2014.

Raheb, Mitri and Fred Strickert. *Bethlehem 2000: Past and Present.* Heidelberg: Palmyra, 1998.

Raheb, Mitri and Suzanne Watts Henderson. *The Cross in Contexts: Suffering and Redemption in Palestine.* New York: Orbis, 2017.

Raheb, Viola. "Reading Micah 5 in Modern Bethlehem." In *Micah (Wisdom Commentary)* edited by Julia M. O'Brien, 65–67. Collegeville, MN: Liturgical, 2017.

Richardson, Don. *Eternity in their Hearts.* Ventura California: Regal, 1981.

Rihbany, Abraham Mitrie. *The Syrian Christ. Second Edition.* London: Andrew Melrose, 1920.

River, Charles, ed. *Bethlehem: The History and Legacy of the Birthplace of Jesus.* Charles River Editors, 2016. Kindle Edition.

Roberts, Alistair J. and Andrew Wilson. *Echoes of Exodus: Tracing Themes of Redemption Through Scripture.* Wheaton: Crossway, 2018. Kindle Edition.

Rogerson, John. "Micah." In *Eerdmans Commentary on the Bible,* edited by J. D. G. Dunn and John Rogerson, 703–707. Grand Rapids: Eerdmans, 2003.

Rutledge, Flemming. *The Crucifixion: Understanding the Death of Jesus Christ.* Grand Rapids: Eerdmans, 2015.

Sacks, Rabbi Jonathan. *Genesis: The Book of Beginnings (Covenant & Conversation: A Weekly Reading of the Jewish Bible).* Jerusalem: Maggid, 2009.

Samir, Youssef. "The Cross and the Power Issue: A Middle Eastern View." In *Arabic Christian Theology: A Contemporary Global Evangelical Perspective,* edited by Andrea Zaki Stephanous, 374–422. Grand Rapids: Zondervan, 2019.

Schreiner, Thomas R. *The King in His Beauty: A Biblical Theology of the Old and New Testaments.* Grand Rapids: Baker Academic, 2013.

Seale, Morris S. *The Desert Bible: Nomadic Tribal Culture and Old Testament Interpretation.* London: Weidenfeld and Nicolson, 1974.

St Paul's Auckland, "O Little Town of Bethlehem," (16 December 2012) https://www. youtube.com/watch?v=bjQDl95tOcU

Sternberg, Meir. *The Poetics of Biblical Narrative: Ideological Literature and the Drama of Reading.* Bloomington: Indiana University Press, 1987.

Strickert, Fred. *Rachel Weeping: Jews, Christians and Muslims at the Fortress Tomb.* Collegeville, MN: Liturgical, 2007.

Sugirtharajah, R. S. *Asian Biblical Hermeneutics and Postcolonialism: Contesting the Interpretations.* Maryknoll: Orbis, 1998.

Thompson, William McClure. *The Land and the Book: Or, Biblical Illustrations Drawn from the Manners and Customs, the Scenes and Scenery of the Holy Land.* New York: Harper & Brothers, 1871.

Vermes, Geza. *The Nativity: History and Legend.* London: Penguin, 2006.

Volf, Miroslav. *Exclusion & Embrace: A Theological Exploration of Identity, Otherness and Reconciliation.* Nashville: Abingdon, 1996.

Walton, John H. and J. Harvey Walton. *The Lost World of the Israelite Conquest.* Grand Rapids: InterVarsity Press, 2017.

Welby, Justin. "Foreword." In *God Is Stranger: What Happens When God Turns Up?* by Krish Kandiah, Kindle Locations 54–98. London: Hodder & Stoughton, 2017. Kindle Edition.

Witherington III, Ben. *Revelation (New Cambridge Bible Commentary).* Cambridge University Press, 2003.

Wright, Christopher J. H. *The Mission of God: Unlocking the Bible's Grand Narrative.* Nottingham: IVP, 2006.

Wright, Tom. *Revelation for Everyone.* London: SPCK, 2011. Kindle Edition.

Ziegler, Yael. *Ruth: From Alienation to Monarchy (Maggid Studies in Tanakh).* Jerusalem: Maggid Books, 2017.

Printed in Great Britain
by Amazon